This book is to be returned on or before

THE HISTORY
OF
ORNAMENT

ALEXANDER SPELTZ

THE HISTORY
OF
ORNAMENT

Antiquity to Modern Times

STUDIO EDITIONS
LONDON

The History of Ornament
was originally published in 1915
by A. Schumann's Verlag, Leipzig,
under the title *Das Farbige Ornament aller Historischen Stile.*
This edition is published by Studio Editions
an imprint of Bestseller Publications Limited
Princess House, 50 Eastcastle Street
London W1N 7AP, England

Copyright © Studio Editions, 1989
All rights reserved. This publication may not be
reproduced, stored in a retrieval system or transmitted
in any form or by any means electronic, mechanical,
photocopying, recording or otherwise without the prior
permission of the publishers.

ISBN 1 85170 175 3

Printed and bound in Hong Kong

CONTENTS

LIST OF PLATES

INTRODUCTION

It was in the early stone age that man began to decorate his utensils and tools by means of a primitive art. Pictures of animals carved in horn or bone by means of pointed stones have been found in several caves in France and Switzerland. They exhibit, in spite of their primitive character, a remarkable understanding of the special features and movement of those animals. Sculptures of animals and human beings have also been discovered, although of very primitive workmanship. Opinions differ as to whether drawing or sculpture were the first art form of man. Even in this early period of art man already began to employ colours, as is proved by series of painted mammoths, aurochses, reindeers and horses found in the caves of Les Eyzies in France and Altamira in Spain. These paintings are remarkable accomplishments for such a primitive culture.

In the late stone age man left the caves and inhabited round or square huts of loam walls covered with thatch. Towards the end of that period we find primitive dwellings built on piles in the middle of lakes, so-called lake villages, the inhabitants of which, however, appear to have undergone a long stagnation in their development compared with the inhabitants of the land. The period produced those noteworthy stone structures known as barrows, cairns, menhirs, cromlechs and stonehenges (fig. 1), especially in the Celtic countries. It is a strange fact that the drawings of this period are fewer in number and decidedly inferior to those of the

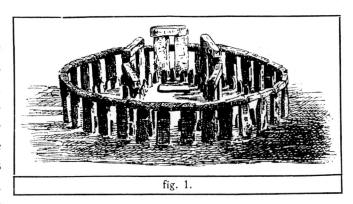

fig. 1.

early stone age. It seems that the realism in representation was dropped and a new kind of art sprang up, tending towards the use of ornaments, while in handicraft an improved sense of form and even a taste for objects of personal adornment developed. In examining the pieces of plaited work found in the Swiss lake villages, we can easily trace in them the natural origin of ornamental designs. By means of differently coloured switches man developed even a coloured ornament. Similar designs, consisting of dots, lines, zigzags, crosses, curves and circles predominated in ceramics, but it

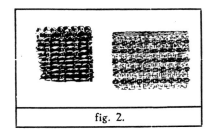

fig. 2.

1

is not very likely that the ceramic art took its ornamental models from the textile art. Simple as this purely linear art is, it became the standard for textile art.

Especially in southern Europe towards the end of that period a sort of 'band-ceramics' was developed, a continuous design with a carved strip at the top and the bottom.

The transition from the stone age to the iron age took place in different periods for different tribes, gradually spreading from the Orient across southern Europe to the north of it. Drawings found dating from the third and second millenium are on no account to be compared with those of the earliest periods in artistic achievement and perfection, although as a kind of hieroglyphics they afford a distinct idea of reality. Weapons, tools, gems, etc., however, clearly manifest an improvement in the formation and ornamentation, as well as in occasional employment of polychromy. In ornamental art a certain system was developed, mainly consisting of bulges in rows, spiral lines combined with each other more or less artistically, zigzags, circles, etc. In this way a style came into existence which for a millennium predominated in the whole of Central Europe.

According to Karl von den Steinen and many other experts the Bakairi ornament in fig. 3a represents the scale-pattern of a certain fish (Mereshu-fish), fig. 3b the pattern of bats, fig. 3c the scale pattern of another fish and fig. 3d the uluri, a triangular loin-cloth. The fact that all these figures are filled in with black strengthens the impression that they have been taken from a concrete object. This certainly must overthrow all theories about the prehistoric geometrical ornament. Is not, for instance, the volute, which we find so often in prehistoric art and even later on in historical art, very likely to be an imitation of that spiral line which we see in so many chonchifera, such as snails, and which has been the model for the Ionic capital?

It is more likely that the artists of the stone age made their sketches from studies of nature rather than composing their ornaments artificially of geometrical figures, be they ever so simple. And furthermore it is to be supposed that there have been copyists who copied these orginals, and in doing so deformed them in such a way that originally purely naturalistic drawings finally were changed into purely ornamental motives. As we can trace in still existing primitive races the origin of their whole ornamental art, it must be possible to find the origin of the so-called geometrical ornament of prehistoric art.

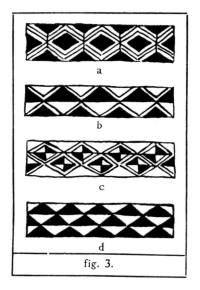

fig. 3.

There is reason to believe that the development of art has progressed from the naturalistic to the geometrical motive, for the ornament cannot be a primitive thing either in its principles or in its mode of application. It must be the result of the naturalistic drawing of an object. Even if we admit that the Peruvians at the time of the discovery of America were much more cultivated than the modern Indians in Central Brazil, it is almost certain that their ornament had the same origin as that of the modern Indians in Brazil. The advanced textile art of the Peruvians does not make it likely that the figures exhibited in the fabrics are only the produce of an inferior artistic ability.

The rise of this type of ornament out of the original naturalistic ornament can easily be traced in the remains found on Crete.

ANTIQUITY

Egyptian ornament

Egyptian art has served as a model for the forms of art to many other nations, especially to the Achaeans and Greeks. The objects found on Crete, at Mycenae, Tiryns, etc. have revealed the transition form from Egyptian to Greek art in a most decisive manner.

The oldest Egyptian wall-painting known to us was executed in black, white and red, and represented life on the Nile in rather primitive drawings. It showed a strict schematism, which is to be traced through nearly all the periods of Egyptian art. This schematic art we may term court-style. Egyptian painting was either plain or relief painting, and the Egyptian relief must be included in the art of painting, for it was not intended to represent sculpture, but simply distinct outlines of paintings. Those outlines were mostly incised so that the picture was on a level with the surface of the wall; sometimes, however, the background was also engraved, the picture then resembling a bas-relief. At any rate, the style of drawing and the execution of painting were the same.

The perspective employed by the Egyptians in representing human figures is strange, or rather there is no perspective at all. Every part of the body is represented as it shows itself most characteristically. Head, arms, legs and feet are always represented in profile, eyes, shoulders and chest *en face,* the lower part of the trunk in half side-view, the hands are invariably shown with the fingernails visible, whereas the feet are drawn from the inner side to avoid shaping the toes.

Moreover, this schematic mode of representation was subject to various principles of style, e.g. outstretched arms and legs were always opposite to the spectator, perhaps in order to maintain the distinctness of the drawing. Besides, the said court-style required that all persons represented should look to the right-hand side, and if that was impossible, the figure was simply turned around with all its details. This strict schematism seems to have been laid down as a principle already in the prehistoric period, as can be seen in the oldest monuments. We must consider, however, that the artists of the earlier times had not been quite so restricted by the court-style as those of the later epochs, but were still experimenting.

In the wide-ranging reformation in religion and art under Amenophis II Echnation the court-style was suppressed, and a more popular art was elevated to the rank of state art. But the reformations of this sovereign were too far-reaching and already under his successor Haremheb (1350–1315 BC) reaction restored the former conditions. Schematism again became the prevailing form of art, and originality and free artistic aspiration disappeared. Only the technique of painting had derived advantage from these changes, as the reliefs in the temple of Setho (1315–1292 BC) clearly show.

The main employment of painting in Egypt was in the decoration of walls and ceilings, columns, capitals, grooves, channels, etc. In many tombs of the pyramids the walls were covered with rosy-red polished granite, which in most cases was varnished with a coloured glaze, while the hieroglyphs were painted with opaque colours on the rough background. But here, however, we already find occasionally coloured tiles of faience about 2–3 cm in size as wall-covering, probably the first occurence of tessellated walls. Walls of sandstone or bricks were plastered with stucco, which was impregnated with a kind of varnish. Even paintings on the wood or linen always had a thin ground of gypsum. The paintings on the shafts of columns and on capitals, smooth in the beginning, in later epochs gave way to hieroglyphic reliefs with painted reedings at the base of the columns. Gradually all parts of architecture were painted, whereas in the earlier periods contrasts existed between painted and unpainted surfaces.

The Egyptian art of wall-painting was based on the idea of imitating carpets hung on the walls, as the purely decorative edgings prove, and we must assume that there has been a textile model, as in so many other parts of architecture of various styles. The painting of ceilings also was an imitation of the coloured fabrics suspended from the ceiling, as was usual in tents in Antiquity. Later on the ceilings were decorated with stars on a blue background, probably in imitation of the starry sky, or with eagles, scarabs, the zodiac, etc. As motives for coloured decorations as well as for sculpture served the lotus flower, the attribute of Isis and the symbol of the germinating power of nature, nymphs, papyri, reed, branches of palms, etc.

Just as conventional as the drawing was the selection of the colours; strong colours with distinctly marked, mostly incised, outlines were applied next to each other without any shading. The colours employed were red, blue, yellow, black, white, green and brown. Sometimes they were applied to a black background, but generally a bright one was prefered in order to make the hieroglyphic characters more visible. Men were suggested in red-brown, women in yellow, the later being considerably smaller. The Egyptians were so far advanced in their textile art that they were capable of producing fabrics in pronounced polychromy and with figures depicted in them.

Babylonian-Assyrian ornament

The Assyrians introduced polychrome ornamental brickwork. The walls of Assyrian buildings were nearly always composed of air-dried bricks. As plaster does not protect such walls sufficiently against the weather, it was only natural that they were covered with a more solid material, and for this the Assyrians used either alabaster tiles with reliefs, or glazed clay tiles. The ornamentation of these tiles opened a large field for polychromy. Floors were also paved with baked clay tiles.

Similar to Egyptian art, the Babylonian-Assyrian art was bound by convention and therefore must at last necessarily become as lifeless as Egyptian art. Usually figures were yellow on blue or white backgrounds. Green was only occasionally used for objects of lesser importance, black for details, red and white for ornaments. These colours sufficed to mark out especially the patterns of garments or purely decorative details. In the earlier works of Nimrud strong dark colours were preferred, blue, white and black, while in the era of Saragon a pale blue predominated with white, yellow and orange, whereby a more elegant effect could be obtained.

Phoenician ornament

The Phoenicians were merchants rather than artists, and did not develop their own national art. On their voyages through all the then known world they introduced the Oriental works of applied art and they became very important mediators. The influence of Oriental art on the archaic Greek art is especially due to the Phoenicians. The Phoenicians had a flourishing industry, the products of which they traded together with Egyptian, Babylonian and Assyrian works of art. They therefore had a great influence on the development of classical art. The penetration of Etruscan art with Greek elements is mainly due to them. Phoenician works of art show a mixture of Egyptian and Babylonian elements. However, the Phoenicians were famous for their glass, which resembled Egyptian glass, and for their metalwork, especially their shallow embossed and engraved silver bowls.

Persian ornament

In the remains of Persian art not many national elements are to be found. The Persians brought artisans, mostly prisoners of war, from countries they had conquered into their main cities, where they constructed the magnificent buildings planned by the Persian kings. It is obvious that this introduced especially Egyptian, Babylonian-Assyrian and Greek elements, which in the end drove the national art, not very important itself, into the background. While at Persepolis reliefs predominated, at Susa wall-coverings of glazed tiles were preferred, an ornamentation probably taken from Assyria and Babylon. There are two well known friezes of glazed tiles: one of stalking lions between rich bands of ornaments, resembling the well known lion-frieze of Babylon, and the other of striding warriors, five by five between two pillars, on a bluish-green ground. Here the artist dropped the Egyptian mode of representation, half complete view, half profile, and the garments show a freer drapery. In spite of its monotony this long frieze is imposing. These works show a great technical ability and a still more flourishing sense of colours than the Babylonian-Assyrian works.

Aegean ornament

AEGEAN CERAMIC ART

In Aegean art the ceramics are especially noteworthy, which on Crete reached an exceptionally high state of development. The polychromic Aegean art is scarcely inferior to the Greek one. The oldest specimens of the Neolithic are fragments of black burnt clay with simple incised figures, often filled in with a white material. There are no curvilinear ornaments; among the rectilinear ones triangles with inferior lines, crooked bands and comb-patterns occur most frequently. The period following the Neolithic has been called early Cretan or early Minoic (derived from King Minos of Crete) and is divided into the first and the second early Minoic style. The works belonging to the first were coloured black, with the decoration, incised in earlier periods, painted in white; there are also vessels with glossy black bands on the ground of clay. In the second style curved and spiral lines predominate, executed in a durable white. Some of the vessels of this style apparently were formed by means of the potter's wheel.

Polychromy appeared in Cretan art in the early middle-Minoic period. It employs besides the traditional white a pale red, crimson and orange. Some of the vessels are also decorated with ornaments, on a polished bright background of clay, others, like those of Grecian make, have incised designs. We must regard this period as a time of transition, partly corresponding to the early Minoic and neolithic period, partly introducing new ornaments which were not fully developed until the late Minoic period. This period is conspicuous by a fresh and vivid naturalism, and we also come across relief-like ornaments. The surface of the vessel was either divided into several horizontal or vertical sections of equal size, which were uniformly filled with ornaments, or it was decorated by a broad strip around the vessel.

The products of the late middle-Minoic period (Kamares period) are distinguished by an original polychromic opalescence of white, red and yellow on a glossy black background. The same colours were always employed whether they were suited to the object represented or not. The form of the vessels shows, compared with older ones, a definite further development and refinement.

A conventional vegetal ornamentation with richly interlaced vegetal forms took the place of the linear ornamentation of former epochs. The chief aim of the artists of this period was more an elaborate system of coloured lines than the imitation of nature to achieve a decorative and polychromic effect. In this period the natural object is worked over to such a degree that vegetal motives become linear.

After the development begun in earlier times had reached its summit, a great change in the whole of Cretan art came with the substitution of monochromy for polychromy. As in Japanese art, drawings began to represent a quick impression in a lively but rather formless style without exact details. While in former periods the brilliancy of colours was the chief object of the artist, in monochromy the drawing itself became the most important feature. Egyptian motives were introduced into Cretan art, but these foreign motives were absorbed by the Cretan art.

A new element entered Cretan art in the first period of the late Minoic style by the introduction of maritime fauna and flora. In the beginning we find a number of animals and plants drawn from nature in a strictly naturalistic manner, but later on these objects were copied from earlier works. The naturalistic motive thus became more and more subordinate, so that at last the manner of execution made it impossible to recognize the original model. The only recognizable object was the cuttle-fish. Other models may have been the nautilus, a sea-slug, and among fish especially the dolphin. Ornaments of lesser importance were corals and, among plants, several kinds of seaweed. Besides those naturalistic ornaments there are paintings of a more conventional kind, mostly schematic representations of vegetal origin, e.g. the continuous spiral line arranged in various patterns.

Excavations on the mainland have brought to light objects of another period of art coinciding with the late Minoic period: varnished vessels from the tombs of

fig. 4.

fig. 5.

fig. 6.

fig. 7.

fig. 8.

fig. 9.

Mycenae, which are in stark contrast to the pale vessels then used on the mainland. Research has shown that the age of the tombs of Mycenae is coincident with that of the 18th dynasty in Egypt (1570–1305 BC), and that there has been communication with that country.

In the second period of the late Minoic style a blackish varnish was used for vessels. The ornaments were distributed over the surface of the vessels, but did not cover all the surface area. Although this style shows some symptons of decline in consequence of the exaggerated schematism, it nevertheless represents one of the high points of Cretan art.

Cretan ceramic art was unparallelled compared with that of the Greek mainland and the Greek islands. Cretan art created the magnificent Kamares style with its brilliant colours and its unsurpassed workmanship at a time when the artists of the mainland and the neighbouring islands still painted simple patterns in subdued colours on technically inferior vessels. Later, when the Cretan palaces were destroyed, Cretan art was absorbed by the Cretan-Mycenaean culture.

The use of animal and vegetal objects of the sea as models for ornamentation, in pure naturalism at first, then in rigid and lifeless forms, is a characteristic of Aegean art. This feature of ornamentation is easily explained in a race which was in constant and intimate contact with the sea; it is to be considered as an independent autochthonous part of Aegean art, which does not occur in the Egyptian and Babylonian forms of decoration.

Another kind of ornament not found in the earlier Egyptian or Babylonian decorations is the spiral, the main motive of Cretan ornamentation. It is possible that the volute of prehistoric European art may have been taken from Aegean ornamentation. The alterations and variations which the polyp has undergone in Aegean ornaments raises the question whether perhaps the volute may be the imitation of a rolled-up arm of a polyp (figs. 4–8). The golden link of a necklace represented in fig. 9 was surely developed after the model of the head of a polyp and is perhaps even the original model of the Ionic capital, which was used in Phoenician and Egyptian ornamentation long before the development of Ionic art.

There is no doubt that Aegean art was influenced by Oriental and Egyptian elements. Egyptian works of art signed with the royal seal of the 12th dynasty (about 2200 BC) have been found on Crete, and at the entrance of the large oasis of El Fayum in an early Egyptian settlement of the 16th century BC, early Cretan painted earthenware has been discovered.

AEGEAN FRESCO-PAINTING

The main colours of Aegean fresco-painting are white, red, yellow, blue and black. As in Egyptian art, men are depicted in red, women in yellow. The original red hue of the wall becomes the background of the picture. Later on a predilection for contrasts of colours prevails. In most cases red and white, yellow or blue are put next to each other and the ornaments are usually painted red on yellow or black on blue backgrounds. Ornaments on white backgrounds are mostly red, on light red backgrounds black.

The paintings of Knossos have a certain canon of colours, which is the same in all periods of Mycenaean art. Every decorated wall has a specially marked base, while the rest of the surface is delimited above and below by horizontal bands of ornaments or is divided into several friezes. Here the horizontal wooden beams seem to have played an important part, there are no vertical divisions of the wall, not even in the corners. A single wall does not form a chromatic artistic whole, but only a part of the decoration of the whole room. This is a peculiarity of Cretan-Mycenaean wall-painting. The upper part of the wall consists of pictorial friezes and bands of ornaments. Most of the friezes found show figures in full size and have a small white strip above and below to divide the coloured areas from each other.

The ornament in Cretan-Mycenaean wall-painting is merely a decorative band to frame the surfaces. It is a pure ornamentation of surfaces with scales, intertwined wreaths, zigzags, etc. Not only walls, but also floors and ceilings were decorated with fresco-paintings. Of some importance is the influence of mural painting on ceramic art, which later not only copied motives of fresco-painting, but imitated the whole system of decoration.

Greek ornament

POLYCHROMY IN ANTIQUE ARCHITECTURE

The polychromy of antique architecture has its origin in the Orient, where the exuberant nature induced man to apply its richness of colours to his own creations. Assyrians, Babylonians and Persians used polychromy in their buildings, the air-dried bricks of which they covered with coloured tiles in order to protect the exterior walls against the weather, and so combined the useful with the beautiful. They also used fresco-painting to decorate interior walls.

Polychromy was perhaps used on the largest scale in the architecture of Egypt, where the interior walls and relief-ornaments of temples, pyramids, tombs, palaces, etc. were decorated in colour. To the Egyptian his temple meant the world; its columns represented gigantic lotus flowers, papyri or palms and were painted to give the impression of a forest. The ceiling, blue with yellow stars, represented the sky.

Excavations have shown that Greek temples were at least partly painted. The discoveries at Olympia give, in spite of their belonging to different periods of the Doric epoch, evidence of a system of principles of polychromy. The regular occurence of the same colours on corresponding parts of architecture accounts for a conventional execution of polychromy in Greek architecture.

There is no doubt that the Greeks took form as well as colour from the

Egyptians, the latter, however, as a means of concealing the inferiority of the materials they used and of improving the appearance of buildings by painting in combination with sculpture. On the other hand we must not forget that in the brilliant light of the Greek landscape, which was rich in colours itself, large masses of marble in its natural colour would have been painful to the eye, so that the Greeks probably would have been led to polychromy even without the Egyptian example.

In general all details projecting from the background were painted, as was the background of the reliefs, whereas the walls of the cella, the columns, epistyles and mouldings had the natural hue of the stone, which only rarely was covered with a sort of wax varnish. In the Doric temple the abacus of the triglyph and the coping of the architrave were always painted, while this was not always the case with metopes without reliefs and the oval mouldings of the Doric column. The front of the epistyle was sometimes decorated with a continuous ornamentation of tendrils or gold plates or with gilt inscriptions. Below triglyphs were fillets fastened with falling gilt drops and little green palmettes. The top band had a delicate red or green meander, the triglyphs a deep azure tone. The figures and ornaments of the gable were painted in natural colours, as was usual for sculpture, on brown-red, blue or yellowish backgrounds. The cymae were decorated with friezes of golden leaves, the smaller parts of the oval mouldings with heart-shaped leaves, edged with red lines and furnished with ribs, on a green background. The lion's heads of the cyma, the ornaments of the acroteria and the antefixes were painted either in deep colours or gilt.

Usually the ceiling of the portico had the same colour as the walls, the edgings of the coffers of the ceiling had gilt chaplets on a blue or green background, the horizontal surfaces had a design of red meanders, the fillets of the oval mouldings projecting coloured leaves or egg-mouldings, the background itself golden stars on blue ground.

The earliest Greek temples (e.g. those at Assos, Pergamon, Aegina, etc.) were built of porous limestone or tufaceous trachyte and it was impossible to apply the colour directly to the stone. It was necessary to prepare a basis of a fine white stucco, which on some works is in a good state of preservation even now. But stucco being rather frequently in need of repair, it was substituted by marble, which, as it required no special preparation for painting, soon became the exclusive material of Greek architecture.

In Greek polychromy unbroken colours, that is to say unmixed colours without any intermediate shades, were used: blue, red, green, yellow and gold (for terra-cotta vessels also brown and black), pink was used for fleshtones, and light green and violet for garments. The use of deep colours, probably an imitation of the Egyptian polychromy, is accounted for by the fact that most of the painted parts were at a considerable height and would otherwise have produced hardly any effect.

Not only the Doric, but also the Ionic and Corinthian buildings of the earlier periods were partly painted, as finds at Olympia and in the Acropolis at Athens have proved. Even whole Corinthian capitals were painted.

There is no evidence of a Roman polychromy similar to the Greek one. The Romans tried to attain a certain polychromy by the use of differently coloured materials in combination with bronze. The same principle was now and then applied in Greek sculpture, but most of these works were of marble and painted.

At Pompeii the painting of statues seems also to have been customary, as a wall-painting from there shows (fig. 10), representing a female artist who paints a herma according to a sketch lying before her. The museum at Naples has numerous painted works of sculpture from

fig. 10.

Pompeii. The parts representing flesh seem to have been unpainted, only a varnish of oil and wax was applied to them in order to obtain an aspect like that of the human skin. But the eyes were painted, analogous to the setting in of a special material into statues of bronze.

In Greek sculpture flesh was represented in ivory, and garments were gold or bronze. It is very likely, by the way, that the classical art may have taken the painting of sculpture from Egypt. For example, a wall-painting has been found which represents Euté, the head sculptor of the Queen Mother Tey, painting the statue of the princess Beekt'eten in the tomb of the administrator of Tey (fig. 11).

fig. 11.

Similar to the Greek temples, parts of the Etruscan temples were decorated with figurative wall-paintings on interior and exterior surfaces. White was frequently used. As far as evidence proves, the whole timberwork of the temple was painted, partly to conceal the roughness of the material and partly to protect the wood against the weather.

POLYCHROMIC GREEK TERRA-COTTA

The glazed colours of antique terra-cotta are in a better state of preservation than those painted on stone. In regions where marble was rare, especially at Olympia and in Sicily, terra-cotta was very often used for the covering of the wooden or stone cornices of the roofs.

The Doric temple doubtlessly developed out of timber structures. It was only natural to cover the wooden parts with terra-cotta as a protection against the weather, especially those of the coping which were very much exposed to it, while the ends of the beams and the triglyphs were protected by paint and by the projecting mouldings. The copings were given protection by putting three-edged cases of burnt clay over the modillions and nailing them to the rafters. But as the projection of the mouldings was not sufficient to protect the columns against the weather, stone was introduced as building material for the columns. But even later, when the whole temple was constructed of stone, the builders continued to nail terra-cotta to the limestone as formerly to the wood. It was not until experience had taught them that good stucco was as secure a means of preservation that they substituted terra-cotta plates with painted plaster. In the earliest times roof-tiles also had a covering of black, brown or red varnish (fig. 12). In the 6th and 5th centuries BC, terra-cotta was fired lightly, later on more strongly.

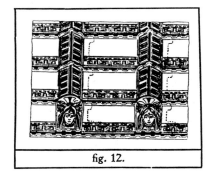

fig. 12.

In the use of ornamentation local particularities and a certain chronological development can be discerned. The characteristic ornament of the casings is a design of interwined bands, generally double, rarely single, edged with astragals, resembling the tori of the columns. The eyes, round which these bands are wound, are not arranged diagonally, but vertically, consequently where two bands meet empty wedges are formed which are filled in with decorative palm-leaves, while in other cases the bands cover each other without blank spaces. The height of the single or double ornaments was regulated by the height of the decorated surfaces. The astragals edging the surfaces and those of the cymae were painted either with horizontal or transverse band-ornaments or, as at Selinunt, with scale-ornaments; the bases of the casings were decorated with coloured strips, tri-angles, rectangles, meander patterns, etc. Tiles at the gutter had mostly band-ornaments, further ornaments of rosettes and wavy lines, later on only meanders.

The visible lower surfaces of the roof-tiles were painted or decorated with meander ornaments. The crowns of the roofs were formed by cymae running all round the building or by a system of tiles. The horizontal line of the coping was interrupted by lions' heads and acroteria. The formation of the cymae in Greece is simpler and more uniformly developed than in Sicily; it uses mostly anthemion ornaments.

The earlier terra-cotta had a subdued brownish-black or brown-red varnish on all exterior surfaces. The various opaque colours, mostly pale orange, white, brown-red and violet, were painted on the varnish, which is why they deteriorate quickly. Characteristic features of this terra-cotta are the heavy plastic forms and the simply constructed geometrical designs of intertwined bands, rosettes, zig-zags, semicircular leaves, etc. The designs were incised and filled in with colour. In later terra-cotta execution was similar, but it progressed from geometrical to freer forms. Instead of the dark background of varnish we find a light yellow tone either as background for the other colours, or painted between them. The design invariably shows a rhythmic succession of two dark tones, brownish-black and red in several shades. In order to get a smooth surface the object was covered with a fine coating of clay into which the design was carved. But in this period (5th century BC) plastic art is much inferior to that in the earlier period.

GREEK VASE-PAINTING

The art of vase-painting differs from the kind of painting described earlier in its monchromatic execution, and in its lack of aerial perspective, chiaroscuro and shading. The representations consist of more or less life-like figures positioned side by side or one above the other; the scene of action is symbolically suggested. The figures are represented either by simple outlines or in silhouette, the muscles, garments and distinguishing details and ornaments within the outlines are indicated by lines. The silhouettes are either part of the natural ochreous or variously coloured background spared out in the black glazing, or are in black glaze on an artificial reddish ochreous background of clay, the outlines being painted in the former case, incised in the latter. But we often find both modes together; apart from the black silhouettes there are sometimes unglazed colours, whereby the monochromatic painting becomes polychromatic. The use of black contours seems to be the leading feature at the peak of that period of Greek vase-painting.

The colours were dull in general, with the exception of black, which was mostly glazed by fusion with metallic oxide. The quality of this glazing naturally depended on the quality of the clay and that of the colours, on the degree of heat and on the length of the firing. This black glazing being easily fusible, it was possible to mark the outlines of the yellow figures in elaborate workmanship whereas the white outlines on black-figured vases had to be incised.

In Greek vase-painting the following types must be distinguished:

(1) Burnt black earthenware, without painting, mostly with a glossy, but occasionally with a dull glaze, with incised or pressed decorations or reliefs, with black or white glazed or unglazed painting on a grey background, consisting of decorations, heads and figures in silhouette etc. This style was especially followed in the Apulian workshops. In the ochreous painting, especially that of the Campanian workshops, the ornaments or figures were in unglazed areas of the background and had black lines within the contours. The yellowish, reddish, or brownish colours were mostly produced by the background itself, but sometimes also by the application of sinapis-red or unglazed red ochre. Adornments and other details were sometimes suggested by white or yellow. Black figures on an ochre background were incised in silhouette and covered with a fine black glazing, but backgrounds of unclean white are also to be found. Decorations of garments were sometimes dull violet and the flesh parts of the figures were white.

(2) Burnt ochreous earthenware either in the natural colour of the clay or with red or brown glazing. The figures were ochre on brown-red backgrounds, the flesh parts being suggested in the colour of the ground, but there also occur brown-red figures on bright yellow backgrounds or black figures with incised

outlines on bright, mostly glazed backgrounds of ochre; in this case the flesh parts of the figures were white, and the garments in parts violet.

(3) Burnt white earthenware with brownish-black figures. These vessels of ochreous clay were covered with white clay and the figures had brown or black outlines. Occasionally the black figures, which were drawn in silhouette, were furnished with brownish-violet ornaments. Some vessels were painted in four, six or even more colours.

Etruscan ornament

The Etruscans, like the Greeks, used polychromy in order to accentuate the outline of their buildings and the reliefs of their sculptures. They also used polychromy on a large scale for decorative purposes, and the great number of Greek vases which were imported seem to have been their models. The best known example of this art is the wall-painting found in one of the Etruscan tombs, copies of which are in the German Archaeological Institute in Rome. The Vatican, Bologna and British Museums also have copies of it, but these do not show all the details of the original. This style of decorating tombs seems not to have existed all over Etruria, but appears to have been confined to certain districts such as Corneto (where 50 tombs have been discovered), Chiusi (about a dozen tombs), Cervetri (four tombs), Vulci, Orvieto, Bieda, Bomarzo, Cosa, Orte, Veii and Vetulonia (one tomb each).

These wall-paintings are never painted on masonry, but on the hewn rock, either directly or on a layer of plaster. As the rock of this region is mostly fine-grained limestone, it was possible to paint directly on the stone. Other types of rock were covered with a thin plaster of lime and sand in order to produce a smooth background. In these paintings, as in those of Pompeii, one can still see the traces of the instruments used in copying the outlines from the cartoons. The areas within the contours of figures were filled in with colour, afterwards the contours were redrawn. The areas between the figures were in most cases unpainted and showed the yellowish tone of the plaster. The main colours were sooty brown, vermillion, cinnabar, lime-wash, ochre, cupric oxide and verdigris, often mixed in order to obtain various shades of colour.

These paintings must not be regarded as pictures, but as decorations, and they followed the conventions of Egyptian paintings. Also, as they were located in dark rooms, they seem to have been intended to be seen by the light of torches rather than daylight. Sculptures were painted with a pigment which probably contained albumen.

These tomb-paintings always represent rooms of the house of the deceased, giving reason to believe that the houses of the Etruscans also had wall-paintings, as stated by Pliny. The subjects of these paintings were mythological scenes and scenes from the Trojan War, while in the tombs the leading motive seems to have been a banquet with couples on couches in various positions. The subjects exhibit in general a naive realism, the people depicted playing musical instruments, singing, dancing, etc., but there are also pictures depicting the existence after death, representations of Greek and Etruscan legends, portraits, landscapes, and there is even a picture of a complete butcher's shop.

The Etruscan wall-paintings belong to various periods. Those found in the tomb of Campana at Veii, probably painted towards the end of the 4th century BC (Veii was destroyed in 396 BC), are badly drawn, but curious to say with a correct knowledge of anatomy, which strengthens the impression that these pictures were copied from Greek vases. This Graeco-oriental style seems to have been in general vogue in Etruria from the 6th century BC. This period is succeeded by that of the painted clay tiles of Cervetri, which exhibit scenes of Etruscan life, but do not altogether deny a certain Greek influence either. This style is gradually supplanted by the introduction of Tuscan elements, and after red-figured Greek vases had been imported (about 460 BC) a pure Tuscan style was at last developed. Thus an Etrusco-Greek style came into existence as a consequence of the combination of Greek influences with pure Tuscan elements, which is to be found especially in the wall-paintings of Corneto, Chiusi and Orvieto. This particular style produced towards the last period of Etruscan art purely mythological compositions, which are distinguished by better, more realistic drawing and finer colouration. But in spite of the fact that there is the occasionally correctly drawn head, a good profile, an expressive and eloquent physiognomy, a well chosen and combined group and a well drawn drapery, the artistic execution in these paintings is but mediocre and sometimes rather careless. The frequent repetition of various subjects raises the suspicion that there might have existed certain models, probably taken from Greek vases, which were widely used. These paintings give us the opportunity to trace the development of Etruscan art step by step, but their value is more historical than artistic.

Roman ornament

ROMAN FRESCO-PAINTING

Pliny states that he saw paintings predating the city of Rome, which allows the conclusion that Italy must have had a very old tradition of painting. Besides these indigenous paintings there were foreign ones, especially in the era of Augustus. According to Vitruvius fresco-paintings were executed on a treble layer of plaster, which in turn was covered with a treble coating of stucco consisting of carefully sifted marble dust and slaked lime. Finally the uppermost layer was polished with marble dust and, still moist, painted. The sizing for ancient fresco-painting was gum, tragacanth, animal sizing, albumen or milk (in Egypt the blood of the hippopotamus), or wax with an admixture of oil or resin if a polish was to be produced. Sometimes whole pictures with their stratum of stucco were separated and inserted into newly plastered walls. The so-called fresco secco system still used in Italy now, in which dried stucco is moistened, was already in vogue in antiquity. For retouching distemper paints were used with strong adhesive substances such as albumen, honey or milk.

Pompeii and Herculaneum are the only places where complete Roman frescos have been preserved. But fragments of frescos in the imperial palace in Rome exhibit the characteristic features of the transition from the second to the third Pompeian style, which, strange to say, has not yet been found at Pompeii itself. A certain freedom of execution and an abundance of artistic ideas is shown in the paintings of the imperial palace. The festoons of fruit hanging between columns with religious motives and wavy bands are original motives which give a room a dignified and solemn aspect. A calyx decorated with sea-dragons, however, seems to be an unsuitable base for a supporting column, especially if it has altogether lost its tectonic purpose through decorations of inorganically added heads, tendrils and bands. In colouration the principle is to apply lighter and lighter colours the nearer they are to the top. Lights and shades of the panels are suggested by white or black lines. Areas painted in similar or unharmonious colours are always separated by lines of another colour.

ROMAN MOSAIC

Mosaic is the reproduction of drawn ornaments or pictures by a composition of coloured stones, pieces of burnt clay or glass, etc. in order to produce durable decorations of walls or floors. The various methods of this process are most easily traced in Pompeian art. The most primitive mosaic is a floor of pounded bricks and lime, into which patterns of square cut stones are pressed; the surface is then smoothed and polished.

The mosaic comes from the Orient. The earliest European mosaic, in the temple of Zeus at Olympia, dates from the first half of the 4th century BC. Favourite and mostly very naturally executed subjects for the floors of dining rooms were remains of food, sweepings, etc. Another prevailing style was a mosaic of pigeons sitting on the brim of a basin. Later on even the most difficult artistic compositions were reproduced in mosaic. Mosaic probably originated in Alexandria when walls were completely covered with marble so that no room was left for paintings, which consequently were moved to the floor. This was imitated at Pompeii, although the walls there were covered with painted stucco, and the mosaics were probably the work of craftsmen from Alexandria. Especially famous is a large mosaic at Pompeii which represents the battle of Alexander the Great at Issos. During the conquests of the Romans this art spread to the Roman provinces, and magnificent Roman mosaics have been found especially in the Rhineland. Most remarkable are the mosaic floors divided by ornamental frames into circles, ellipses, squares, rectangles, etc., each decorated with an ornament of plants or figures. The small pieces of marble or glass were embedded into a cement of lime and oil on a mortar of brickdust with a layer of lime and gravel below. The later mosaics are technically, but not artistically better than the earlier ones. From the 3rd century BC gold foil was used in mosaics, whereby this art achieved a still higher appreciation, especially as the gold and the brilliant colours of the glass, which later on was used instead of marble, the art of execution and the durability of the mosaics easily excelled painting. In the course of time figurative representations progressively gave way to purely ornamental decorations in mosaics.

ROMAN ENAMEL

It was discovered in antiquity that when pounded glass was heated in a furnace it formed a glassy flux, or enamel, which could be used for ornamentation. As large surfaces of enamel cannot be bonded and colours run into each other, thin strips of metal were soldered onto the surfaces which were to be decorated, and so the so-called cellular enamel, or cloisonné enamel, was gradually developed.

The green enamel, which in Roman enamelling is always to be found under the vitreous paste, seems to have been used to form a better bond between metal and the material laid on. The vitreous pastes employed in enamelling very likely had the same combination as the glass used in mosaic. The colouring pigments were copper for red, blue and green, and lead, antimony and uranium for yellow and orange. The Romans did not use special chemical compounds but natural minerals or earths in colouring the glass without knowing the active materials in them.

POMPEIAN FRESCO-PAINTING

There is no doubt that the Pompeian artists painted from Graeco-Alexandrian models, although certain peculiarities indicate that their models were not the Greek original paintings, but somewhat incorrect copies. Nevertheless these artists were highly accomplished not only in conception and composition, but also in form and colouration.

The Pompeian wall-paintings were always frescos. Four periods of style are to be distinguished:

(1) In the era of the republic the whole wall was divided into horizontal rectangles in order to imitate marble facing. The base was a projecting plain plinth, and the middle and the upper parts of the wall were divided from each other by a projecting moulding. The marble-like painted surfaces of the rectangles projected and the junctures were incised.

(2) Later on those rectangles became more varied and larger and fictitiously projecting columns made the room appear more spacious than it really was. In the centre section of the wall persons and objects were represented in a realistic manner; the top section of the wall was painted white and blue, representing the open air, strengthened by painted parts of architecture, tree-tops, etc.

(3) Under Augustus, coincident with the introduction of foreign motives, especially Egyptian and oriental ones, the imitation of marble facing was discontinued. The wall was divided into three sections by small columns, pillars or objects resembling chandeliers, etc. Very wide walls had an additional division of the two outer sections. The central sections were framed, executed as carpets or niches and mostly furnished with a picture. On the side-faces were often floating figures, on the upper part fantastic figures or objects. The plinth was occasionally omitted.

(4) After the first earthquake in 63 AD, when Pompeii was rebuilt, we notice a rococo-like decline of the art, a wild, fantastic confusion of all possible forms of architecture, vegetal decorations, figures, views of the interiors of houses and pictures with a good many drawings of men and animals. The imitation of marble re-appears, but with receding surfaces and projecting junctures.

However, we cannot assume that these four styles followed one another strictly chronologically. There was an earlier and a later period with the 'second style' probably between them. It is difficult to date Pompeian frescos by the style. However, we know that those paintings were executed by a guild, as it were, of painters of succeeding generations, who had been trained in the style which had spread from Alexandria. Although not all these painters were Greeks, the Pompeian frescos are classified as Hellenistic.

The style of the frescos at Herculaneum is about the same as the Pompeian style, but its development, though the same in the main features, took another course. The execution is more antique, and the painters were superior artists. The colours are more brilliant and richer, the ornamentation is more ingenious and the design more expressive.

Polychromy of the Buddhist cave-temples

The promotion of Buddhism to state religion by King Asoka (276–240 BC) was the beginning of a new era of Indian art quite different to the former Vedic-Brahminic one. It lasted until the 8th century AD, when it was replaced by the Neo-Brahminic art. With regard to polychromy the wall-paintings of the cave-temples, especially those of Ajantâ (6th century AD), represent the highest accomplishment of this art and at the same time an authentic document on the development of Buddhism, the rise of the teacher and philosopher Buddha to a divine dignity and the mode of life of that time. In most cases the founder of the religion is represented in a strictly conventional manner, as in China and Japan, but sometimes also as a human being living among men. The same style, the same symbols, the same decorative details and the same manner of composition are to be found in the Buddhist paintings of Nepal, China, Japan, Burma and Java.

As nearly all modes of painting employ the same technique, in the Egyptian and Etruscan tombs as well as at Pompeii and Herculaneum and at Ajantâ, they necessarily must correspond to each other to a certain degree; thus especially a fresco of Ambrogio Lorenzatti (14th century AD) shows in colouration and execution a striking resemblance to the wall-paintings of Ajantâ. From the exact mode of drawing in the latter, especially the representation of the hands in the most difficult positions (fig. 13), we may infer an advanced artistic training of the creators of these paintings. The feet, however, are somewhat neglected; the exaggeration of the women's hips and bosoms is common to all Indian sculptors.

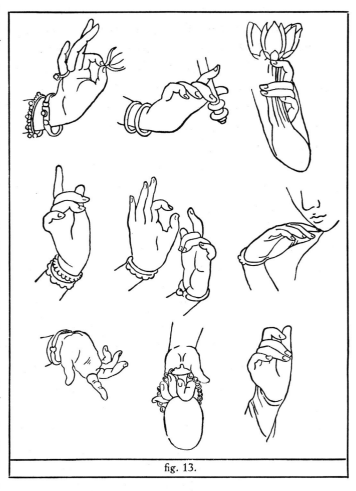

fig. 13.

The execution of these paintings is a mixture of painting in distemper and fresco. A plaster of clay, cow-dung and trap-dust about 20 mm thick was applied to the rock. Then a thin coat of gypsum was laid on with a coarse brush and smoothed with a trowel. The drawing was traced or powered on this smooth surface. The outlines were drawn in brown or black, the paint was applied and the details were executed.

In some of the temples white bright lights were obtained by scratching off the colour and laying bare the white background.

Early Christian ornament

Coincident with the expansion of Christianity in the first centuries AD a new art form developed which was different from the classical one. It was, however, not an entirely new style, but rather an adaption of classical art to the new Christian philosophy.

As the existing examples of early Christian art represent only a small proportion of the works created at that time, we are no longer justified in attributing to early Christianity an aversion to art in general. On the contrary, the habit of decorating coffins, burial-places, churches, houses and religious and profane objects manifest a pronounced antique culture. The early Christian works of art are therefore part of the whole of late antique art.

The symbolical motives in early Christian works of art are the monogram of Christ X and P, A and Ω, the fish, the dove and the anchor. Sometimes we find representations of the figures of Christ and the apostles in life size or as busts, scenes from the life of Christ or from the Old Testament and representations of everyday life with pious inscriptions and symbols. The early antique manner of using human figures and scenes was gradually substituted by the purely ornamental and decorative principle of the early medieval period, but this change is by no means to be considered as a decline but only as a change of taste.

There is no doubt that in the first centuries of imperial Rome, Italy was the leader in all forms of art, but the east of the Roman empire soon developed other centres of art, which were mostly also the centres of early Christianity, such as Syria, Palestine, Asia Minor and Egypt. Moreover, with the transfer of the imperial residence to Byzantium in 330 AD another centre came into existence which soon excelled Rome in pomp and magnificence. Consequently early Christian art was divided into two main branches, a western and an eastern one, but the latter soon lost the largest part of its sphere to the advance of Islam. Early Christian art in Byzantium developed later into the so-called Byzantine art.

When Christianity was adopted as a state religion in 330 AD the eastern centres of culture played an important part, especially Egypt. So many remains of early Byzantine and early Christian art have been found in Egypt that it caused an entirely new interpretation of the early Christian period in the history of art. Especially the numerous textile remains discovered in the necropolises of Achmin (Panopolis), Antinoë, Fayum, Sakkarah and Bawit put antique textile art in a new light. The products of the native (then Christian) population are called Coptic. The decoration of Coptic fabrics does not consist of woven patterns, but of gobelin-like weaving. In ordinary weaving two systems of threads called warp and weft cross each other, while in gobelin-work the coloured thread only extends as far as the design requires and then is cut off and knotted at the back. The background is mostly a yellowish-white canvas, the design an embroidery of coloured or purple woolen yarn. The remains which have been found are parts of garments with sumptuous and colourful decorations. Fabrics decorated with religious representations did not have a special religious purpose as liturgic garments for the clergy were unknown, but they were frequently used to decorate churches, in which case they were generally silk. The finds at Achmim prove that silk was worn even in the earliest times of the empire. Garments made entirely of silk were very rare at that time, but trims on linen, where the linen threads were substituted by silk threads, occurred very frequently.

All textile work of later periods was based on Roman classical rather than Egyptian art. The Hellenistic textile ornament of Alexandria became after the transfer of the imperial residence to Byzantium a mixture of declining classical and early Christian or Byzantine art. Polychromy gradually displaced drawing.

The era after Justinian is characterized especially by wild and hard forms and glaring colour schemes combined, however, with a somtimes remarkable chord of colours. The colours of the background are purple, brownish-violet and red, usually madder, and the colours of the ornaments are indigo, violet-blue, sky-blue, golden yellow, orange, green and black.

Late Greek ornament

At the time of the decline of classical art a new characteristic style was developed in Greece and her colonies on a classical basis with oriental influences. Specimens of this have been found in the so-called Treasure of Petrosa (Rumania). Although the existence of runic letters on a smooth bracelet proves that this treasure has been in the possession of Germanics, it must be considered as a product of late Greek art. It is probably the booty of a Teutonic tribe invading eastern Greece which was buried when the tribe retreated.

THE MIDDLE AGES

Late classical Germanic art

In the 4th and 5th centuries the countries from the Black Sea to Spain, from North Africa to Britain, which for centuries had been under the influence of Roman culture, were invaded by Germanic tribes from northern and eastern Europe. These tribes soon founded their own states, most of which, however, were only short-lived. Combined with the progressive advance of Christianity, a new direction in art produced independent new forms. A study of the ornaments of the period following the migration of the Germanic tribes shows that a new barbaric or Germanic style took to some extent the place of, and influenced, antique art.

Before their invasion of the Roman empire the Germanic tribes had adopted an art of their own which then combined with Roman classical art. On the other hand, the late antique east and west Roman elements were subjected to barbarian influence. We can only assess this Germanic art from the tools and utensils which have been discovered. The barbarian style is manifested above all by the exclusive use of solid gold for utensils, whereas in classical art silver had been used for utensils and vessels.

The technical and ornamental characteristics shown in all objects found are tangible proof that an original Germanic art existed at the time of the migration. One of the characteristics is the mosaic-like adornment of gold implements and jewelry with red gems, later with thin red and green glass plates. Another characteristic considered as being originally Germanic and used in innumerable variations is the ornament of interlaced and interwoven bands, often adorned with heads of animals. It may be assumed that the cellular mosaic works of that period are either east Roman originals or Germanic imitations of them. The craftsmen in the areas conquered by the Germans continued their trade despite the retrogression of culture and the general devastation. Furthermore, in the 5th century the Goths, for instance, were no longer barbarians, but doing their utmost to uphold the old Roman culture. The exisiting workshops became schools for the Germanic craftsmen, as is proved by numerous glass vessels found in the Rhineland, Italy, France and England. The glass vessels of this period, however, lack the elegant shape, fine outline and practical construction of antique glass.

Tribes which were less willing to sacrifice their nationality for a higher civilization brought a touch of barbarism to the classical style, particularly in their metal works and even in the most costly examples of cellular mosaic, found mostly in transalpine excavations. The 8th century reliquary of Burgundian origin at St. Maurice in the Swiss canton of Valais is an important example of this art. This work differs from the Byzantine-like works of the Goths and Langobards above all in the uncouth treatment of cellular ornaments and early classical design.

Roman art had a greater influence in northern Italy and Spain. The gold treasure discovered at Fuente de Guarrazar is a beautiful collection of votive crowns, which were hung above altars. Nine of these crowns are in the Museum at Cluny and three in the Armeria Real at Madrid. The crowns appear to have been made in Spain, probably by Byzantine goldsmiths.

Byzantine ornament

The early Christians had only very little appreciation of art and considered it to be the chief stronghold of paganism. Therefore, when Christianity did begin to adopt art, this had to be different from classic art. The art of the old catacombs was a purely symbolic one, without scenes of martyrdom or portraits, but using mythological decorations and representation of country life. The mystic symbols of anchor, fish, pigeon, etc. were very frequent. This art had a delicate and poetical character: Christ as a good shepherd leading his sheep to pasture, the immortal soul among the flowers of paradise, the allegorical figures of Psyche and Orpheus, Daniel and Jonas. With this simple-minded symbolism the easy temper of the oriental philosophers was mixed in some liturgic representations. Up to the early 4th century Christian art was a simple, familiar and popular one.

When Christianity became a state religion at the beginning of the 4th century art began to flourish to an extraordinary extent. Divine service now no longer took place in gloomy catacombs, but in splendidly decorated basilicas. The interior walls were covered with marble and glass-mosaics, capitals and ceilings were gilded, and the floors were covered with coloured marble-mosaics.

Christianity entered into a close relationship with the government, which protected it in return and made it a strong instrument for its purposes. Christian art became the official art and, aided by the emperor and the court, it quickly attained the most exquisite splendour.

When the imperial residence was moved to Byzantium the political centre of the Roman empire shifted to the east, which now was also the centre of Christianity. In consequence the new art, in contact with the oriental civilisations and Hellenism, was able to develop strongly.

However, classicism was not the only fountain-head of the new Christian art. Persian art, which under the reign of the Sassanids (226–651 AD) excelled especially in enamel work and tapestry, also influenced Christian art.

Thus three elements contributed to the new Christian art: Christianity, Hellenism, and the Orient. Only gradually and influenced by Constantinople there came about certain uniformity, before the characteristic features of

Byzantine art were to be seen. This art, however, is not be considered an exclusively religious art, it is also a profane one.

Because of its geographic position, Constantinople was especially suited to combine the influences of the Orient and Hellenism, and although the new style had its cradle in the centres of art of that time, Asia Minor and Egypt, it was consolidated only in Constantinople. The new imperial residence, the immense number of new buildings, the luxury of the court and the continuous contact with the masterworks of Hellenism created a great and powerful movement of art which merits the name of Byzantine art.

Among the countries in which the origins of Christian art are to be sought, Syria from the 4th until the 6th century is of special interest. Syria was a rich country with a dense population and a flourishing industry and had trade connections from Spain to Persia, India, Central Asia and even China. Syria also had many centres of learning for science and theology. With this background Christian art was bound to develop vigorously. In spite of the great influence of Greek art and the long Roman reign paganism had not been eradicated completely in Syria; on the contrary, this gave a quite special colour to Syrian Christianity and its art.

Among the old cities of antiquity Alexandria occupied a prominent position as the centre of commerce in the Mediterranean. Although Alexandria was the capital of Hellenism, it had Egyptian traditions and the victory of Christianity favoured the renaissance of Egyptian national art. Thus in the 3rd century Coptic art came into being and, especially in Upper Egypt, held out well against the Hellenism of Alexandria. It is true that the first elements of Coptic art were Hellenistic ones and remained so for a long time, but the inspiration and technique were purely Egyptian. With the aid of Christianity it gained its highest point in the 5th century. As the Syrian art, Coptic art was a combination of Hellenic elements and oriental motives, until it finally became fully oriental.

Alexandrine art was essentially a decorative one that above all sought for picturesque detail and realism. Christianity soon claimed this picturesque art, and the churches erected in the 4th and 5th century exhibit many profane motives: birds and flowers, hunting- and fishing-scenes, landscapes of the Nile valley, architecture similar to that in the Pompeian frescos and pictures representing everyday life and ornaments. Yet Alexandrine art did not cultivate the picturesque alone, but also realism. All those characteristic, expressive portraits found in Fayum show to what a high degree Hellenistic art was able to depict human features. It is the same art that we find in the encaustic pictures of Mount Sinai and in the mosaics at Ravenna, and it certainly had a great influence upon the development of Christian art, especially upon that of historical painting. The origin of Byzantine manuscript-painting is also to be found in Ptolemaic Egypt.

Byzantium owes its taste for polychromy no doubt to the Orient. Many ornamental motives, as well as processes for relief-work substituting form for colour, came from Persia. The development of polychromy in Byzantine art is truly remarkable and is a fundamental aspect of its art. For exteriors alternating strata of stone and brick, marble facing and faience application was employed, whereas in the interiors marble and glass-mosaics predominated. Byzantium owes its picturesque style of painting to the Hellenistic Orient, but its historical and monumental style to the Orient proper.

During the reign of Justinian (527–565 AD) Byzantium art began to stagnate, and after the emperor's death it became progressively more decadent as all energy was needed to defend the empire threatened by the Slavs and the Persians. In the 7th century the flight to Rome because of the advance of Islam was so great that Rome almost became a Byzantine city. This Byzantine influence was so strong that Greek custom spread over all of Italy, the festivals of the Greek saints were celebrated and even Greek names and the Greek language were adopted. Art was obviously influenced by these developments and Byzantine art of the 7th century can only be judged in conjunction with the art in Italy at that time.

In the 8th century the depiction of human figures and the veneration of icons was proscribed and many religious paintings were destroyed, but after the icono-clasm the 9th century saw a renaissance of art in the Byzantine empire, called the second golden age of Byzantine art, as a consequence of the political renaissance under the reign of the Macedonian emperors (867–1056 AD). As always in the renaissance of an art, people turned back to antiquity and tried to breathe new life into Byzantine art. At the same time they tried to imitate the opulence of Arabian art in Baghdad, Damascus, etc. This renaissance of Byzantine art ended suddenly with the conquest and sack of Constantinople by the crusaders in 1204, after which Byzantine art vegetated until the conquest of the city by the Turks in 1453.

BYZANTINE GLASS-MOSAIC

In early Byzantine glass-mosaics the long rows of saints at first glance appear to be very similar to one another, and most of them seem to be designed following the same model; they are only distinguished by age and colour of beard and of hair. There are three types: angels, prophets and apostels, and among each of these types there is youth, maturity and old age. Sometimes different saints seem to be portraits of the same person. However, closer examination shows distinguishing characteristics: the bishops and monks have a bony, rough face, a clumsy body and a monotone and weary expression, while the angels with their handsome figure, rich dress and free and stout bearing have a face that radiates beauty. In contrast to the old Greek type here a new one appears with slit eyes, hooked nose, and long hair falling to the shoulders. These figures show the influence of classical Greek masterworks in their movements, bearing and clothes. But beside these purely classical inspirations we also find other influences, first of all that of the church which tended to glorify ascetism, separate beauty from art, and impose austerity and solemnity on the pictures. But cosmopolitan Constantinople also gave artists exciting and interesting new models. The spirit of innovation also prevailed in the compositions. Within the bounds fixed by the clergy, artists tried to create new and original works of great elegance and harmony of composition, mobility and richness in colouring.

In the 6th century figures dressed in white had been set against a blue background, but in the time of the Macedonian and Commenen emperors a gold background became characteristic, with a richer colouration of the figures and exclusion or diminishing of landscapes.

Progress was also made in technique and the use of pigments which allowed richer and different colour combinations. Complementary colours were placed next to each other and this technique of contrasting of complementary colours and setting strong colours against the gold background produced marvellous results.

Fine examples of Byzantine mosaics are in St. Mark's in Venice, which had close connections with Byzantium. St. Mark's was built under the doge Domenico Contarini between 1063 and 1095, but the completion to its present state took another four centuries. Unfortunately many of the Byzantine mosaics in Venice were destroyed or damaged during the Renaissance. There are also rich mosaics of Byzantine origin in Ravenna and in Sicily, which was a Byzantine province for three centuries.

BYZANTINE ENAMEL

The art of enamelling is very old as is proved by finds made in Egypt. The Egyptians decorated their jewellery with gem stones mounted between narrow strips of gold, but they also used coloured glass-flux instead of gem stones. Byzantine art and science adapted the ancient art of enamelling and created a particularly characteristic art in the time of Justinian. In Byzantine enamelling thin strips of gold were soldered onto a gold base following the outlines of the design and forming a cell for the glass.

The decoration of Hagia Sophia and the manufacture of jewellery and utensils for the imperial household under Justinian gave the enamellers, who it appears came from the Orient, great scope. There was no state monopoly in enamelling but the emperors established special workshops at their court. The art of Byzantine enamel flowered between 850 and 1000.

The Byzantine enamels have a background of gold level with the surface of the enamel, or an enamelled background which is either richly decorated with multi-coloured designs or of a monochrome emerald green, often with close scroll-work. It appears that the Byzantine artists only used gold as the base for their enamels. As the iconographic rules prescribed the dress of saints to be monochrome and without any design, the artists increased the folds of the garments.

The skill and style of the Byzantine enamellers was so highly regarded by their contemporaries that the miniaturists soon began to copy them. The painters imitated enamel work by painting the areas within the outlines in one shade rather than using tones, which is impossible in enamelling where colours cannot be mixed within a cell. A fine hatching with gold replaced shades and folds of drapery in paintings. At the apex of Byzantine enamel even Italian painters and mosaic artists imitated in their wall murals and mosaics the folds formed in enamels by the golden lines.

The cross of victory in the treasury of Limburg Cathedral, the older parts of Pala d'oro and pieces in the treasury of St. Mark's in Venice are examples of the flowering of the enamelling art of the 10th century. However, with the decline of the Byzantine empire in the 11th century after its loss of all possessions in Italy, North Africa and Asia Minor, Byzantine enamel declined from art to merely handicraft. Finally, in the 13th century, there was no longer any demand for Byzantine cellular enamel because by then pit-enamel was successful in competing with it.

All the enamel produced in the Roman empire before the 6th century was either pit- or barbarian enamel. Depressions were beaten into the metal or chiselled out of it and filled with a coloured glass-mass. In pit-enamel, a pit was created for each colour and the metal strips separating the pits were retained, whereas in barbarian enamel the separating strips were omitted. Since pit-enamel was easier to produce it gradually replaced the Byzantine cellular enamel.

BYZANTINE MINIATURE PAINTING

However important Byzantine monumental art, fresco-painting and mosaics may be, one cannot assess Byzantine art fully without the large number of illustrated manuscripts that have been preserved. In contrast to the decoration of churches, which was supervised by the clergy, there was considerable liberty in manuscript painting, which has a more individual and profane character. At the time of the iconoclasm in the 8th century artists turned to illumination, which in the 9th and 10th centuries saw a revival following the old Alexandrine models together with classical influences. This new miniature painting created works in much larger variety than those of the high art. The artists of the 9th and 10th centuries copied works from the 4th to the 6th century, but comparing different copies of the same model we can distinguish quite evident differences which prove that these artists did not copy mechanically but endeavoured to accommodate the old models to the taste of their time. The artists of this renaissance exhibit anatomical knowledge which created correct modelling and exact drawing. Generally there are no close relations between illustrations and text; the illustrations very often even remain incomprehensible without a reading of the text, and were probably often suggested to the artist by a clergyman.

After the iconoclasm the victory of orthodoxy in the mid-9th century produced a great theological and monastic movement. The triumph of orthodoxy could not, however, stop the advance of the new renaissance, and the taste for a literary and profane art, which had always been opposed by orthodoxy in Byzantium, prevailed. The artists working for the court and for the aristocracy went constantly farther back to classical models, so that the manuscripts of this period have a prevalence of antique figures, mythological scenes and classical allegories which, although transformed according to Byzantine taste, cannot deny their classical origin. The iconoclasts had given to later generations the taste for sumptuous ornamentation which in the manuscripts of the Macedonian epoch is shown in garlands, animals, birds and elegant initials. But profane art fell progressively under the influence of orthodoxy, which forced it into rigid, inviolable forms which remained until the fall of the Byzantine empire.

BYZANTINE SILK TAPESTRY

Silk was already known in China in the 4th millenium BC, and its use generally spread in the third millennium, but for reasons of political economy it was only allowed to be exported as a finished fabric. It was brought via Ceylon and Turkestan to the West and traded for ivory, precious stones, etc. to the Persians and Phœnicians, who sold it to the Egyptians and Greeks. Although silk drapery then was decorated in various colours, yet its principal value consisted in its brightness and lightness. Not until the 4th century BC did non-woven silk yarn reach Europe, whereupon within a short time large quantities of silk fabrics were woven to European taste. Because of its high price, silk was mostly used only as a trim on linen or cotton fabrics. Pure silk was only worn by the wealthiest and highest classes of society, for in the third century BC silk was still paid for in gold weight for weight.

Only after silk worms had been smuggled to Europe in the mid-6th century did silk manufacture become wholly independent from China, and silk became progressively cheaper. With the technical improvements of the loom more and more richly ornamented fabrics were produced which, however, in an inverse ratio to their splendid colours became worse and worse in their design.

At the time of Constantine the Persians under Sandor II invaded the empire and brought weavers from Mesopotamia to Susa, who now developed the Sassanian silk manufacture which had flowered in earlier periods. But this Sassanian textile art adopted the Roman, Greek, Egyptian and Syrian style since it depended on exporting its products to the Occident.

The emperor Justinian made the prospering silk industry into a state monopoly, and all existing workshops became imperial establishments, which explains why the design and ornamentation of Byzantine silk fabrics became to a certain extent monotonous. Byzantine silk was generally used in the Occident until the late Middle Ages.

During the 7th and 8th centuries silk manufacture developed in Arabia and with its particular Arabian ornamentation and splendid polychromy even served as a model for the Greek silk weavers. Sicilian-Saracenic silk manufacture, too, rose to a high art and its products were used all over Europe.

At the time of the transition from classical to Byzantine art silk fabrics showed in design and colouring reminiscences of the dying Roman-Hellenic art. The colour of silk drapery then was white upon black, seldom black upon white, with tones of grey, brown and light pink. When Christianity became a state religion the figures became somewhat stiff and Christian symbols were used.

When the imperial capital was moved from Rome to Byzantium the blending of Roman art with the colourful oriental art resulted in a polychromy that dominated especially in garments. The principle of oriental art to effect more by splendour of colours than by drawing was mainly responsible for raising the value of damasks of both linen with silk threads woven in and pure silk.

But design became crude and colours became progressively more gaudy up to the 11th century, and the motives were enlarged in order to mask the decline in the standard of drawing. Nevertheless, even with its excessively coloured compositions, silk weaving of that period must still be considered an art. The increase of colouring is surely due to the Arabian influence, principally since the conquest of Egypt. Especially characteristic in the Byzantine-Arabian textile art is the prevalence of yellow (Allah's favourite colour), and the complex intricacy of lines.

South Italian Romanesque frescos

At the end of the 9th century when Byzantium reconquered southern Italy and transformed it to a 'New Greece' both in language and in religion, and even after Byzantium lost southern Italy again, this Greek influence remained under the reign of the Normans and the house of Anjou until the 14th century. Monks, who settled throughout southern Italy, lived either in large monasteries or in isolated cells built into rock. The centre of these hermitages was an underground chapel decorated with pictures. The close contact with Greece, the long Byzantine reign and the extensive trade with the Orient and with the Greek colonies there resulted in the development of a distinctive school between the 10th and 12th century, which reminds us of Byzantium not only in its inscriptions, but also in its style and iconography. The artists' aim seems to have been to decorate the small chapels as if they were large churches. Many cells contain pictures from different periods. We may perceive small differences in style and technique, but not in inspiration. However, there is one significant difference between the pictures from the 11th and 12th centuries and those from later epochs: the former ones principally have a distinct lack of colour; they were painted mainly in neutral and blunt colours, almost monochrome.

German Romanesque

ENAMEL ON COPPER

During the migration of the Germanic tribes cell mosaic was used to decorate metal: flat, mostly red or green, stones and flat glass were mounted in gold cells. Examples of this art are the gold shallow cup in the treasure of Petrosa (Romania), a great number of circular buckles found in Germany, Childerich's sword and the Visigothic votive crowns of Guarrazar near Toledo. But this cell-mosaic need not be considered a barbarian imitation of cell-enamel since Byzantine artists worked in cell-mosaic even at the flowering of their enamel art. In France and in Italy cell-mosaic was substituted by cellular enamel in Charlemagne's time, whereas in Germany no examples from this period have been preserved or found. Not until the Greek princess Theophona's marriage to the German emperor Otto II in 972 did Byzantine gold enamel reach Germany. Soon after her arrival a work shop for cell-enamel following Byzantine models was established in St. Benedict's Monastery at Trier. The chief work of art produced here was the Echternach Codex, made under the empress' direction.

After the Saxon dynasty, which had always protected Byzantine art, had died out in 1024, this art declined before in the first half of the 12th century the domestic enamel on copper reached its highest point.

The ecclesiastic goldsmith's art of the Rhineland in the 12th century worked exclusively in pit-enamel, in which a depression is hammered into or cut out of a copper base. The colours are separated by several fillets left in the plate or soldered onto the plate. The difference between Byzantine and German enamel art does not lie in the different techniques, but in the material: in Germany copper was used instead of fine gold as used by the Byzantine artists. Consequently the terms of gold-enamel for Byzantine art and copper-enamel for German art would be more apt than the terms cell- and pit-enamel.

In enamelling on copper the transparent glass-fluxes which are possible on gold or silver have to be substituted by opaque glass-fluxes. Since copper is much cheaper than gold, the base plate can be much thicker, which helps in forming the pits. Of course the reduction in the price of the metal also secured a better market for Rhenish enamel, even though there was severe competition between the Rhenish workshops and those in Limoges. Both Limoges and Cologne seem to have developed quite independently from each other. The difference between their products lies in the ornaments alone, not in the colours.

The centre of German copper-enamel was St. Pantaleon's Monastery in Cologne. Only the Meuse school in France, managed by laymen, may be considered superior to Cologne for its chiefly figural works. The best master of copper-enamelling in Germany during the Middle Ages was no doubt the Benidictine monk Friedericus in Cologne.

Friedericus' earlier works were executed on a gold base, but his later ones were on enamel ground, and the ornament had to be fixed by a metal fillet to separate it from the enamelled background. Consequently the whole ornament had to be modified, and as a supplement to the former oak- and thistle-leaves, leaves with smooth and more rounded outlines were introduced. For this the intricate Romanesque figures of leaves and tendrils with their broad ribbon-like stalks were well suited. Artists began to melt glass-fluxes of various colours in the same pit without fillets. The shading from dark blue to light blue and white, from blue to green and yellow in the works produced at Cologne was so well done that it could not have been executed better by an illuminator. In this technique all the colours were applied at the same time, and any unevenness of the surface was smoothed out by the application of a colourless transparent glass-flux. This produced that clear brightness of polish and softness of gradation of colours which so many enamels from Cologne excel in.

The principal artist of the Meuse school was Godefroid de Claire, a Walloon; consequently this school cannot be included in German applied art, although the lower Lorraine then belonged to the German empire. This school had a strongly marked character of style, which is especially shown in its figural enamels.

Another artist was Magister Nicolaus of Verdun. Only two of his works still exist: the head-piece of the altar in the Chapter House in Klosterneuburg near Vienna (dating from 1181) and St. Mary's shrine in Tournay (dating from 1205). The former consists of 51 large panels (six of which were added when the altar was enlarged in 1329) arranged in three ranks one above the other, showing scenes from the life of Christ and from the Old Testament. The principal strength of this master lies in his drawings. The figures appear in gilt on a blue background of enamel, the rest is enamelled in various colours in the usual manner of the Lorraine school. This work is of high artistic importance, especially for the power of expression, the hardness of gestures and the beauty of the garments.

The school of Aachen shows the influence of both the Cologne and the Meuse school. The main works of this school can be dated precisely, beginning with the completion of Charlemagne's shrine in 1215 and ending with the completion of St. Elizabeth's shrine in 1249. One of the characteristics of this school is the filigree work richly trimmed with gem stones.

Pit-enamel on copper continued in Germany until the 14th century, when it was supplanted by enamelling on silver, which had been developed in Siena and Paris before 1300. Transparent enamelling on silver in a shallow relief is more precious, but still durable, than German Romanesque copper-enamel. People now were no longer content with a design engraved with lines. By flat modelling with carefully planned graduations they tried to make a perfectly plastic image, the effect of which was augmented by transparent glass-fluxes covering the whole design. This type of enamel developed gradually from copper-enamel with the Gothic goldsmiths' preference for silver, for which transparent glass-fluxes could be used.

GLASS-PAINTING

Because of the rapid increase of mural paintings in Romansque churches drapery became unsuitable for covering the windows. Furthermore, people wanted pictures in the window spaces, too, and so glass-painting was invented. Lead-framed stained-glass windows are first mentioned in the 10th century. Archbishop Adalbero of Rheims (969–988) is said to have installed in his church coloured windows that were richly adorned with pictures. In the first decade of the 11th century a school for glass-painting was established in the monastery of Tegernsee. The oldest panes which still have stained figures on a white background are those in Augsburg Cathedral. They are attributed to the 12th and 13th centuries, but they probably date from the 11th century, since 12th-century windows usually had a blue background. In France the oldest existing windows are those of the Abbey of St. Denis near Paris, which Abbot Juggerius commissioned between 1140 and 1144. The three large windows on the west side of Chartres Cathedral are by the same artist.

In the 11th century glass used for windows was up to 5 mm thick, irregular, dark green like bottle-glass and the pieces measured at most 12 cm across. Five colours were used for staining the glass: red, blue, yellow, green and violet. Unstained glass, being somewhat yellow, was used for representing flesh tones. The colours were painted on, using a pigment tempered with iron peroxide or manganese dioxide and mixed with oil of turpentine, lavender-water or gum. When heated, the pigments fused with the glass.

Romanesque windows have straight jambs joined by semicircles of varying size. As for technical reasons only relatively small pieces of glass could be used in stained-glass windows, it was necessary to reinforce larger windows by horizontal and vertical iron rods into suitable fields which, however, often affected the composition. Towards the end of the 12th century more liberal interpretations rejected the former narrow schematism. Facial expression gained in vivacity and the postures of the figures became more unaffected. Garments had a lively drapery at first, but later became more stylized. Individual figures in the compositions seem to be separated from each other and appear clearer and more distinct.

Together with the development of Romanesque into Gothic, the style of glass-painting had to be modified, as the narrow, high windows of the Gothic required tall figures.

When the large French cathedrals were completed during the epoch of early Gothic art, glass-paintings were executed in large quantities, but soon after the studios were moved from Chartres to Paris in 1250, glass-painting declined in France, in favour of the production of mosaic-windows made of blue and red glass.

Cologne Cathedral, consecrated in 1322, has fine examples of glass-painting. Duke John I of Brabant, Count Thierry of Cleve and many patricians of Cologne presented glass-pictures to the city. The most common colours are blue, red and yellow, less green, still more rarely violet, and the harmony of colours was strictly observed.

In the 15th century the pillars within the windows were disregarded in the composition, which was enlarged over the whole. Instead of the decorative edges perspective architectures similar to the Pompeian mural paintings were used.

Romanesque tapestry in Scandinavia

According to Norse legends and poems Gudrun wove carpets with representations from life in war and peace for Thor, and Brunhilde used embroidery to depict Sigurd's heroic deeds which for a long time afterwards were represented in Scandinavian tapestries. An example of the high point of tapestry in Norway is an 11th-century carpet measuring 2 x 1.2 m, found when the wooden church in Hedemarken was demolished. Its age can be determined by the arms and parts of armour depicted, which are the same as those in the Bayeux Tapestry that dates from about 1080, and by the Romanesque architecture shown in the carpet.

Later examples of carpets and cushion covers have similar representations but also show animals in the ornamentation.

Medieval ornament in France

MURAL PAINTING

The origin of French mural painting lies in Roman painting, which was predominant in France until the migration of the Germanic tribes. From the traditions of the Merovingian epoch (482–768) maintained in the monasteries a new art developed which gradually gave way to the influence of Byzantine art. The buildings from this epoch were destroyed a long time ago, but still existing manuscripts give information about mural painting of this period.

The earliest paintings show a mixture of pagan and Christian symbolism. For instance, Christ was often represented as Orpheus playing his lyre and taming lions with his music, as a young shepherd carrying a straying lamb on his shoulders, as a phoenix perched on a palm-tree, or as a fish. These allegories became more and more complex and developed to veritable hieroglyphics. For example, newly baptized men were represented by a stag drinking from a spring, by a vine or a mount, faithful Christians by plants, sheep or birds, and the four Evangelists by four streams flowing over the universe.

At the end of the 7th century the Church decreed that realism should replace allegory in representations of Christ's crucifixion, but this edict was not followed at once, and the dying Christ instead of being represented like a man dying in pain was painted as a triumphant youth. Gradually rules were established for the execution of all religious pictures. These rules, although not strictly observed in the Occident, nevertheless ensured a uniformity of style which is characteristic for paintings up to the 10th century. Examples of these rules are:

Adam's creation: Adam a youth, beardless and naked, standing before God who was surrounded by radiant light; around them trees and animals; above this the heaven with sun and moon.

Eve's creation: the paradise as above; the naked Adam, sleeping, resting his head on his hand; Eve emerging from his side; before her God in radiant light, holding her with his left hand and blessing her with his right.

Explusion of Adam and Eve: The paradise as above; Adam and Eve wearing fig leaves flee, pursued by an angel with six wings holding a fiery sword.

Joseph and Mary on their flight to Egypt: Mountains in the background; the Holy Virgin with her child sitting on an ass, looking back; Joseph holding a stick; in the foreground a town with idols tumbling off its walls.

In the time of the crusades painting became highly symbolic: one tree represented a whole wood, a wavy line a cloud and a door was a symbol for a house or even a town. Glass-painting at this time had not yet reached the high state of art of the later periods and mural painting was the predominant art form for decorating churches.

Fig. 14. Examples of geometrical principles used to construct figures in the 13th century.

In the 13th century painting became more independent of the rules for selection of scenes and in their representation and gradually abandoned the old traditions. But as glass-painting developed into a pictorial art form, mural painting soon lost impetus and originality, and often imitated glass-painting. However, mural painting was retained for church vaults and apses, which were decorated with angels or religious scenes, and for interior decoration of castles. Mural painting served not only as decoration, but was also used to inform and instruct: the owner of a castle immortalized his victories in war or illustrated folklore, and the Church used paintings to illustrate the principles of Christian faith.

The artists followed certain practical rules which allowed even lesser artists to achieve the high standards manifested in old paintings. A book in the National Library of Paris by Villard de Honnecourt, an architect of the 13th century, has illustrations showing how the artists of that time constructed their compositions on geometrical lines (fig. 14). Many different techniques were used for several centuries. The main ones were painting in fresco, wax, distemper and oil.

FLOOR MOSAICS AND TILES

The Romans adopted mosaic from the Greeks and developed into a high form of art. Mosaic was extensively used by the Romans to decorate floors; they even had removable mosaic-floors in their tents. The Roman mosaic floors found in France are mostly in the simple but imposing style of early mosaics. But gradually the Romans found mosaics too precious to be used for floors and used them as wall decorations instead of paintings. In order to compete with the painters, the artists making mosaics constantly had to invent new ways to represent the colours of the palette, which finally caused the decline of Roman mosaic art at the same time as the Roman empire fell.

But when Christianity was established as a state religion it adopted mosaic art as one of its principal art forms, and over a period of time the Church raised it to great heights. During the iconoclasm in Byzantium many monks fled to Italy where they perfected mosaic art to such a degree that their models were followed up to the 12th century. The Church adapted pagan temples for Christian service, but the mosaic floors were mostly retained. Soon the façades and interior walls were covered with mosaics as well. The older basilicas had floors patterned with concentric or touching rings, a mosaic style called Alexandrine.

The mosaic floors laid down in France during the early Christian epoch were not works of native craftsmen, but were mostly executed by Italians. However, from the 12th century on mosaic was gradually abandoned as a floor decoration in France, especially with the spread of the Gothic style which favoured floors of lacquered earthenware or encrusted stone tiles, which were cheaper than mosaic but still produced a good effect.

Decorated stone tiles were used up to the 12th century. Cell-enamel as well as mosaic probably contributed a good deal to their development. The design was chiselled into the stone and filled with pitch or cement mixed with pigments. The artists did not use cartoons in the Middle Ages but drew directly on the polished stone.

People knew already in antiquity how to give terra-cotta a bright glaze, principally in the Orient, in the countries of the Euphrates valley. The glaze consisted of an alkaline aluminium silicate combined with a staining metallic oxide, but later floor tiles were mostly covered with a glaze containing lead or tin. The glazed floor tiles used in France from the 11th until the 17th century are usually stained light yellow. Faience tiles were coated with tin oxide which produced an opaque surface like that in Moorish tiles from the 16th century. We therefore have to distinguish between tiles with a transparent glaze that show the baked clay, unvarnished tiles and faience tiles with an opaque glaze. The first two types were used from the 11th until the 17th century, whereas the third was not used in France until the 16th century, but was soon supplanted by marble tiles.

Earthenware tiles, which were introduced in France by the Romans, were superior to stone tiles in being not as cold and less affected by under-floor heating. The oldest varnished tile found in France is from Richard the Impartial of Burgundy's tomb (936 AD) in the Monastery of St. Colombe-les-Sens. Thus the use of lead-glazing dates back to the time of the Carolingians, and it is a mistake to assume that crusaders introduced glazed tiles to France.

In the Middle Ages designs and ornaments were pressed into clay tiles while they were still moist and the depressions were filled in with clay mixed with metallic pigments such as manganese and chrome oxide and yellow ochre. Lead sulphide was used to glaze the tiles.

In the 12th century two types of tiles were used for floors. The older type, tiles with mat or varnished reliefs, was supplanted later by mosaic tiles with vibrant colours, vigour and harmony. The other type consists of monochrome tiles, often placed next to a smaller tile of another colour; black and black-green were characteristic for the latter. Toward the end of the 12th century tiles were mainly decorated with geometrical patterns, and the tiles were laid in oblong rectangles separated from each other by strips of a more subdued colour. In the 13th century individual decorated tiles were used without consideration for the whole design; the green colour disappeared, but brown and black were retained. Although the difference in the tiles of the 12th and 13th century may not be great, the development kept pace with the improvements in architecture. Often four or eight plates formed one ornament. Lilies were used frequently in this epoch. But after the 13th century the ornament in ceramic tiles declined, and this decline of the art is manifest especially in the 15th century.

Italian silk fabrics

Italy produced no figurative carpet tapestry during the Middle Ages, but had a flourishing silk industry. No doubt North Italian silk weaving stems from the Byzantine-Saracenic style which flowered in South Italy and Sicily under the Normans and Hohenstaufen.

During the Middle Ages and up to the Renaissance Italy supplied the whole Occident with brocade, velvet and silk. The early Italian silk fabrics were an imitation of the oriental ones, often even bearing Arabian inscriptions, and only with the development of Gothic art did the Italian designers achieve independence and transformed the Saracenic patterns into western ones in the course of the 14th century.

What first of all distinguishes the silk designs of this epoch from the earlier ones following the Byzantine-oriental style is, besides their naturalism, chiefly a loosening of the fixed division in the ornamentation and the transition to a free arrangement, often almost giving the impression of a landscape. No later epoch of art has such an abundance of motives as that combination of oriental fancy with early Gothic. The Italian designers turned the Saracenic palmette into a tree, and the arabesque into a vine, an oak or a rose, just as they exist in early Gothic German glass-painting and carpet weaving.

Lucca was the leader in this art until the 15th century, and its products were far more famous than silk produced in Venice, Florence, Milan, Bologna and Genoa, but perhaps of lower quality.

Medieval calligraphy and miniature painting

Papyrus was used from antiquity until the early Middle Ages, and many documents of the early kings of France were still written on this material. From the 8th century on parchment was progressively used, and in the 13th century paper made from rags came into use. The first implements for writing were cane imported from Egypt or pencils of various colours, and from the 8th century goose-quills were used. In the time of Charlemagne people often wrote in gold or silver on purple parchment.

Calligraphy and book ornamentation flourished in the monasteries during the era when books still had to be copied by hand. Parchment being very expensive the text was compressed as much as possible and written without breaks; large initials were used to denote a new line. At first initials were black, simple and without decoration, but gradually the use of red and blue ink and gold and silver came into fashion, and illumination became an art. Small pictures relating to the text were drawn in. Thus book ornamentation in Europe developed from simple initials to the art of miniature painting.

THE RENAISSANCE

The Renaissance represents a turning-point not only in history of art, but also in the general history of humanity. Its importance lies first of all in the delivery of the individual from the oppressive attitude of the Middle Ages by the expansion of humanism. The term 'Renaissance', or 'regeneration', indicates the revival of antique forms, an epoch of art which started in Italy at the beginning of the 15th century. This art took the antique forms as a base, but not in a purely imitative manner; on the contrary, Italian Renaissance is a creative and original manifestation of the artistic genius of that nation.

During the Middle Ages the whole intellectual life was governed by the clergy and any scientific research or discovery that was not in accord with the rigid dogma of the Catholic Church was rigorously suppressed. However, with the progressive loss of authority by the Church on one hand, and the awakening interest in antique art and philosophy on the other hand, Italy produced a revolution. The longing for death as a release into a brighter and better after-life, which the Church demanded of the faithful in the Middle Ages, was replaced by affirmation and appreciation of man's existence on earth and the pleasure of the individual in his works, and upon this Renaissance was founded.

The individualism of the Italian Renaissance is indirectly shown in applied art first of all by the fact that a modern study of nature and of man influenced and benefited decoration and ornamentation. This happened quickly because from the very beginning ornaments played an important part in the Italian Renaissance, and because a great number of leading artists were working in applied art. Furthermore, the copying of works and thus the spread of the art was helped considerably by the use of copperpate-engraving and later letterpress printing.

Many motives in Italian Renaissance were taken from antique monumental decoration. Some classical motives had been used throughout the Middle Ages while others had been rediscovered in the 12th century, but Gothic art had never pentrated Italy to the same extent as northern Europe and the artists of the Italian Renaissance went back directly to antiquity rather than develop the Gothic models. The strength of Italian Renaissance lies in this and in the variety of its schools, as well as in the energy and development which led from early Renaissance to Baroque.

In early Florentine Renaissance decoration was suppressed in favour of the static form exhibited in the 'rustica' style of Florentine architecture. In early Florentine work, principally in furniture, the tendency was towards a form as comprehensible and simple as possible, and ornaments were considered trouble-some and superfluous. Consequently the only ornamentation was a strong profiling to increase the effect of the outlines and surfaces.

From the middle of the 15th century there was a progressive tendency towards decoration and joyful ornamentation, manifesting itself in a striving for grace and elegance. This flowering period is especially characterized by the symmetrical arrangement and concentration around an axis and the clear distinction between the surface and its ornament. Into this joyful ornamentation of the early Renaissance the 16th century brought the sweeping reaction of high Renaissance, in which detail was neglected and ornamentation became coarse because of the predilection for over-ornamentation in order to achieve an imposing effect.

Late Gothic art was by no means decadent, and could have developed further in Germany. The taste for the Gothic form was perhaps not a particularly medieval one, but it was founded in the German character generally. As a result there was no need in Germany to give up high Gothic art and adopt the Renaissance art of the Italians, which in any case was quite foreign to the Germans. However, the contrast between Gothic and Renaissance stimulated German artists around the year 1500, and journeys to Italy awakened among German artists enthusiasm for the antique and the Italian styles.

In Italian Renaissance architecture the German artists saw a strict arrangement around an axis, symmetry and harmony of mass and a predominance of the horizontal over the vertical line typical for Gothic art. The ornamentation in Italian Renaissance art with its motives of putti, heroes, sirens, medallions, garlands, acanthus leaves and elements taken from architecture, such as pillars, pilasters, capitals, friezes and arches, overwhelmed German artists. Italian Renaissance art was predominantly a profane art with its portraits, landscapes, scenes taken from mythology and allegorical figures, and purely ecclesiastic art was in retreat. The German artists travelling in Italy were the most influential factor in the spread of the new art, but since there are considerable differences between the Italian and the German way of life, character and talents, it is obvious that German Renaissance is not a straight copy of the Italian one but an independent product, with its own peculiarities and character.

The first half of the 16th century was the period of the great masters of the German Renaissance. The oldest Renaissance work in Germany is a silver altar made by Georg Seld in Augsburg in 1492, now standing in the 'Reiche Kapelle' in the Royal Palace in Munich. A short time later, Albrecht Dürer began to adopt Renaissance ornaments, although he continued to use Gothic ones from time to time. His designs for goldsmiths especially show Renaissance art to its perfection.

Until the end of the 17th century Nuremberg was the centre of German Renaissance art, rivalled to some extent by Augsburg, but gradually the artists moved to the residences of princes who became great patrons of the art. At the same time the Church, too, began again to support the arts.

In France, where political power was centralized, the Renaissance was promoted by the king and his courtiers. The first products of the Renaissance to

41

reach France were works of Benvenuto Cellini and Andrea del Sarto. Later, in 1530, Francis I summoned Rosso and Primstinio to France; they worked principally at Fontainebleau, and founded a special school there. The potter Girolamo della Robbia, too, worked for Francis I and died in Paris in 1566. Under the influence of Catharine de Medici French artists were sent to study in Italy. Among these were Jacques Androuet-Ducesseau, Phillipe de l'Orme, Pierre Lescot, Jean Goujon and Germain Pilou. In France, as in Germany, Renaissance art at first was confined to ornamentation, and only later influenced and changed architecture.

The Netherlands, in close contact with Germany in the 15th century, had a rich flowering of Renaissance art and culture. The most important artists here were Lucas van Leyden, Johannes Vredeman de Vries and Hans Collaert.

Ceramic art of the Italian Renaissance

After the Italian city Faenza had become famous for its ceramics, all ceramic products coated with a coloured tin enamel were called 'faience'. But ceramics were also covered with a transparent lead enamel, often coloured by metallic salt pigments. Italian faience, however, is called 'majolica' after the Hispano-Moorish ware imported to Italy from Majorca. Gothic ornaments show that majolica manufacture existed already in the 12th and 13th centuries, but it seems to have been confined to producing tiles and circular plates for the decoration of church façades such as in Bologna, Pisa, etc. Besides, these products were only semi-faience, or mezzo-majolica, made in the manner of sgraffito, in which the design is scratched out of the coating. But mezzo-majolica did not develop into an art, as is shown by the many 15th-century fragments found.

The development of true majolica originated with the family della Robbia in Florence in the first half of the 15th century. This family produced a great deal of pure faience, but there must have been other studios in Tuscany at that time, as is proved by finds made especially in Florence, Castelfiorentino and Siena, the decoration of which consists of thick, bluish-black or violet enamel on a white ground. From the characteristic mixture of Gothic and Arabian elements we may conclude that this industry was influenced by imports of Hispano-Moorish articles. Representations of Italian ceramics in German and Dutch pictures show that Italian majolica in the middle of the 15th century was highly developed and exported to the rest of Europe.

Faenza is the oldest centre of the industry, and the oldest majolica vessel, dated between 1393 and 1405, is preserved there. The earliest works still have predominantly Gothic and oriental motives, without proper shading, in a strong blue and some violet, green, yellow and brown. These works mainly consisted of apothecaries' jars, jugs, urns and tiles. The flowering of Renaissance ornamentation in ceramics began towards the end of the 15th century, especially in Faenza, Caffaggiolo, Siena and Castel Durante, the products of which excel in quality and design, colouring and figurative and ornamental composition. But from 1530, when the workshops of Urbino dominated ceramic art, figurative painting began to supplant ornamentation to such a degree that utensils were considered to be nothing but a background for painting, until after the middle of the 16th century a change in fashion, also started in Urbino, again favoured purely ornamental painting.

All existing Italian majolica ware of the 16th century must be considered to be purely decorative items used only on very special occasions. The composition is partly original, but mostly follows engravings, especially those by the Venician engravers Marco Antonio, Agostinio Venetiano and Marco Dente, and to some extent German engravings.

In the early Renaissance Castel Durante was an important centre, principally for its works with grotesque and trophy ornamentation and, since 1525, its grisaille painting. Ceramic tiles from Siena excel in richness and elegance of ornaments in the purest Renaissance style.

The majolica manufacture in Venice seems to have had close connections with Faenza, but the characteristic ornamentation of early Venetian majolica can only be explained by oriental influences on style and technique, such as its grey or bluish enamel which, applied as a thick coat, gave a stained effect to the colours, and its oriental flower-tendrils with fine stalks painted on porcelain in blue with white lustre on a grey background. From 1525 on this oriental style was replaced by Renaissance ornaments. The Urbino style was introduced in Venice by Domenigo de Venezia in 1540.

Italian Renaissance jewellery

During the Renaissance an artist usually was painter, sculptor, architect, engraver, etcher and goldsmith at the same time. The first of these artists was Lorenzo Ghiberti (1381–1455), famous for his large bronze sculptures and goldsmith's work. Other important artists who started as goldsmiths were Giovanni Turini from Siena, Michelozzo Michelozzi, who later became a sculptor and architect, and Andrea Verocetio, who became a sculptor in the Vatican and teacher of Pietro Perugino and Leonardo da Vinci. The first artist to have a jeweller's shop was Antonio de Pollajuolo (1426–1498), also famous as a painter, who perfected the transparent enamel on relief ground. The greatest goldsmith of the Renaissance was Benvenuto Cellini (1500–1570) who first worked in Italy and later in France, where he contributed greatly to the growth of Renaissance art.

Most of the existing pieces of Italian Renaissance jewellery are pendants, and the majority of them are attributed to Cellini. Their central motiv is usually a pearl or cameo surrounded by enamelled volutes or figures. In early Renaissance goldsmith's work enamelling predominated, but because of the growing interest in classical gems and cameos the cutting and polishing of gem stones began to be of importance. The first master of this art appears to have been Vittore Pisano, and its principal centres were Florence, Milan and Rome.

Italian book ornamentation

As in the other forms of Renaissance art, Italy took the lead in book ornament-ation, even though the technique of printing from movable type came from Germany and the type foundries in Italy were at first exclusively managed by Germans. Until the end of the 15th century only black letter (Gothic type) was used for theological and juridical works, but the 1465 edition of Lactantius was already typeset in beautiful Livora characters. For a time a semi-Gothic was used as a transitional typeface between Gothic and Renaissance characters. All the Italian book ornaments, however, exhibit the pure classical spirit from the begin-ning. As in Germany, at first all the spaces for ornaments were left blank in printing and were afterwards illuminated by hand. However, because of the high cost of manual illumination this method was soon replaced by the reproduction of ornaments in print, and in the 1570s printers began to ornament books with those splendid initials, ornamental borders and vignettes which were used up to the 16th century, and which excelled especially in the figures of putti, acanthus leaves and flower ornaments.

It is difficult to prove whether woodcuts were first used in Germany or in Italy, but in Italy the techniques of woodcuts and engraving soon surpassed the German ones.

The first printer in Italy who printed books with classical ornaments was Erhart Ratdolt, a German who emigrated and, after having acquired a fortune in Venice by 1486, returned to his native town of Augsburg. One of the most famous Italian printers was Aldus Pius Manutius, who started his press in 1494 in Venice and became famous throughout Europe. However, most of his books were illuminated by hand. Ottavio Petrucci, who had established a press near Venice, was the first printer that used movable type for printing music, but unfortunately only a small number of his publications have survived.

In Milan, the first printing office was established by Ulrich Schinzengeler, a German from Ingolstadt, and Leonhard Pachel in 1477. Boninus de Bononis worked in Brescia from 1481 to 1491, and his illustrated edition of Dante's works is one of the most beautiful products of Renaissance printing.

Stoneware from Oiron

Only a few examples of this faience ware have survived. They have a delicate and harmonious design that seems to have been inspired more by the goldsmith's art than by architecture. These faiences were made between 1529 and 1568 in the castle of Oiron near Thonars by the potter François Carpentier under the artistic control of Helene de Hangest and her husband Artus Gouffier. The finest pieces made under Helene de Hangest's personal management exhibiting pure forms and the characteristic ivory tint date from the period 1528–1537; those of the second period, up to 1563 when her son Claude Gouffier retired from the manufacture, have a more complex form, but show no real improvement on the first period; they often have the letter H in a cartouche and the three interlaced half-moons of Diana of Poitiers. This most promising art died out with the Gouffiers.

These admirable and very rare pieces have been imitated frequently, but without success. Most of the few existing pieces are from the dinner service of Henry II and Diana of Poitiers, and are therefore sometimes also called Henry II faience.

French faience

After the decline of ceramic art in Italy many Italian artists emigrated to France where they gave a new impetus to this art. The Florentine potter Girolamo della Robbia worked in France from 1538. Other Italian potters later established workshops in Lyon, Nantes and Nîmes. The first works of a French artist, Masseot Abaquesne of Rouen, date from 1542 but they are still influenced by Italian faience. Purely French were the works of Bernard Palissy, who in his youth had apprenticed himself to a glazier and glass-painter but drew, sculpted and studied geometry in his spare time and later became a land surveyor. During his travels in France, Flanders and Germany he became interested in ceramics and in 1542 he established his own studio in Saintes. Being a Calvinist he was imprisoned in 1562 but was freed by his patron, the Connetable de Montmorency, and moved to La Rochelle under the king's protection. In 1565 he was called to Paris by the king and worked for Maria de Medici.

The characteristic individuality expressed in his works is probably due to the fact that he was not a potter by trade and therefore developed his own ideas and techniques, one of which was transparent lead enamels. His colours were mainly manganese yellow, cobalt blue, green and yellow. On glazed surfaces he produced wonderful marble effects by running glazes together. His glazes have their best effect on ornamental plates with smooth flat depressions between bindings and tendrils in which the colours flowed together.

Limoges enamel

In Limoges, already famous in the Middle Ages for its pit-enamel, a particular art developed in the 15th century which either was influenced by French glass-painting or, more probably, was imported from Cologne, and which had no connection with Byzantine pit- or cell-enamel.

The best base for enamel is gold, but because of its high price copper was usually used, especially on larger pieces. In copper enamelling the enamel is applied to a smooth surface without fillets or pits. Thus the metal is like the flat background of a painting, but the craft of enamelling does not lie in the artistic composition and performance as in paintings, but in the purely technical dexterity of applying the enamel; consequently the representations in this art were mostly copied from German, French and Italian engravings.

The first period of Limoges enamel, until 1530, comprises Nardon Penicaud's and Jean Penicaud's works, who engraved the outlines into copper and then covered the whole with a transparent enamel. The engraved outlines, visible through the enamel, were traced over with a darker enamel, within them the many transparent and opaque main colours were applied and the finer modelling was executed in gold and white.

Nardon Penicaud was born between 1470 and 1480 and is still documented as a house-owner in 1539. Jean Penicaud was probably his pupil. Both produced enamels of splendid colours which, however, give the impression that technical difficulties had not yet been overcome. The flowering of Limoge enamel came at a later time when enamellers had learned how to simplify coating and knew more about the firing of enamel. This, however, led to a loss in the brilliance of the colours and finally to grisaille-painting. In this style the copper plates were first covered with a dark background of enamel and this was overlaid with a grey one, on which the design was painted in white.

The greatest master of the second Limoges period as well as of the whole art was Leonhard Limousin (1505–1577), whose works show an unsurpassed mastery of colour and design. Henry II appointed him court-painter in 1548, in which capacity he executed, among other works, two large altar tables for St. Chapelle in Paris using drawings by the painter Niccolo dell' Abbate as models. The most prolific of the Limoges artists was Pierre Reymond, whose earliest work dates from 1534 and latest from 1578. Because of the immense quantity of works attributed to him we can assume that not all these works were executed by him personally, but that he had a workshop and pupils. Reymond was succeeded by Pierre Courteys, who executed large-scale enamels. Like Reymond he preferred grisaille-painting. Besides these are still worth mentioning the masters Jean Court, called Vigier, and Jean de Court; the monogram T. C. is also frequently to be met with.

French jewellery

Whereas in Italy Renaissance first manifested itself in architecture, in France it was applied art that first adopted the new art. Francis I promoted Renaissance art by inviting Italian painters, sculptors and goldsmiths to France, among them Primaticcio, Ross Rossi, and Cellini, who of course soon took on French pupils. As is proved by existing invoices the court ordered an amazing quantity of jewellery in the form of pendants, rings, bracelets and medallions, most of which was decorated with figurative representations from the Bible and later from mythology. This jewellery was in the beginning made of delicate relief work with little enamel. In later years, following Cellini's example, it was executed in high relief or even as free-standing sculpture, often wholly enamelled. The most famous French goldsmiths were Vincent du Bonchaz and Colembert in Lyon and Loys Benoist, Gedanyn and Mataurin de Cosse in Tours.

It is most likely due to Cellini's influence that the Italian school of Renaissance ornamentation survived in France until the reign of Henry III (1574–89). After that time more stress was laid on the material value of jewellry than on its artistic merit.

French book ornamentation

France, the cradle of Gothic art, experienced greater difficulties in assimilating the Renaissance than Italy or Germany. Consequently a mixed style of Gothic and Renaissance art was produced which also showed in book ornamentation. But while in Germany during the transition period artists endeavoured to create a German Renaissance from the Italian one, France at the beginning of the Renaissance had no artists who had mastered the new art sufficiently to become rapidly independent of Italian influence. The result was that at first printers were forced to have their ornaments copied from Italian ones. Only under Francis I was a proper French Renaissance created, and especially an original book ornamentation. Although at his accession to the throne in 1518 prints with ornamental decoration were produced, these were only copied Italian or German ornaments. In 1519 Geofroy Tory began to furnish French printers with drawings for their book illustrations, after having studied the new art for two years in Italy. His designs were first used by the printer Simon de Colines. Tory was the first French artist whose work was pure Renaissance without any admixture of Gothic elements, and his designs became classics of French book ornamentation. All the later French artists adopted Tory's style except Oronce Fine, who treated the new art in a quite individual manner.

Printing from movable type was introduced in Paris in 1469 by three Germans, Martin Crantz, Michael Freiburger and Ulrich Gering, whose first works were printed in roman typefaces which, however, were soon displaced by French Gothic faces. By the year 1500 nearly 50 printers worked in Paris. The first printer to produce the prayer books fashionable in France after 1486 was Simon Vostre; he was succeeded by Philippe Pigouchet and Antonie Verard among many others. In these prayer books ornamentation was still in the French Gothic style, mostly executed manually rather than printed. Henry Estienne used ornamental initials of a marked Renaissance style from 1500 on, but these were copies of Italian originals.

When Simon de Colines married Henry Estienne's widow in 1521 and took over the printing office, he on the instigation of Geofroy Tory discontinued the use of Gothic ornamentation and this workshop went over to Renaissance decoration. Oronce Fine also worked for this printing office from 1530. Robert Estienne's brother Charles Estienne also worked as a printer in Paris from 1536 and was so successful that even the court-printer Guillaume Morel (1548–1564) copied his book ornamentation.

After Paris the most important centre for French book ornamentation was Lyon, where printing was introduced in 1473 and took the same course of development as in Paris. The earliest important printers here were Jacques Saccon and Jean Marion who, however, used only copies of German and Italian woodcuts, and the German printer Sebastian Gryphius, who used only German woodcuts. Hans Holbein worked for the Lyon printers Melchior and Caspar Prechsel and Jean Frellon.

German jewellery

Whereas in France the Renaissance was introduced and promoted by the kings, in Germany, where the emperor had little power and few funds, the cities were the principal promoters of Renaissance art, supported by well educated artists and craftsmen. The new art gained a firm footing first of all in Augsburg aided by Nuremberg artists. The artists of that epoch were not only painters or draughtsmen, but also goldsmiths, engravers and etchers, and works made of precious metals were a favourite art form of the German artists of the early Renaissance. Especially noteworthy artists were in Ulm Zeitblom, Martin Schaffner and the Flemings Jan Grossaert, Jean Swart and Pieter Christus; in Colmar Martin Schongauer; in Cologne Bart Bruyn; in Frankfurt Konrad Fyoll; in Aschaffenburg Mathias Grünewald; and in Thuringia Lucas Cranach. In Nuremberg Albrecht Dürer's pupils Albrecht Altorfer, Hans Sebald, Barthel Beham, Augustin Hirschvogel, Hans Schäuffelin and Georg Penz worked as goldsmiths. In Augsburg the leading artists were Hans Burgkmair and Hans Holbein the younger, whose designs were by far superior to others of that time.

The development of style is best seen in pendants. There were pendants for hats and berets as well as pendants for necklaces and ear-rings. In the Middle Ages such pendants had religious motives, but in the Renaissance mythological or historical figures, later also figures of animals were used. Pendants were often given by princes as a sign of favour and such pendants were the equivalent of modern orders and decorations. Medals, medallions or cut stones were worn on chains around the neck. Ear-rings originated in the Orient and were common in countries with close contact with the Moors and Arabs, for instance Spain and Sicily. In Germany ear-rings were less common and were worn only by women.

Jewellery for neck and chest consisted of chainlike decorations which, however, in time became over-ornate and covered the whole body down to the knees with a net of gold chains. A broad chain with links decorated with enamel or gem stones was often worn across the chest. A special type of these chains were the bridal chains which usually had heraldic motives.

For belts chains were often used, the larger links of which were decorated either with a uniform pattern or with different patterns arranged in a rhythmic sequence. However, leather-belts, often covered in velvet and decorated with gold embroidery, buttons, metal mounts or pearls, were more common. Buckles were usually gilded or silvered bronze.

Buttons at this time were elaborately decorated and used either functionally or as pure ornamentation of garments, hats and caps. It appears bracelets were unusual in the Renaissance, but rings were common and, gloves being indispensable, the rings were worn over them or the glove was cut to reveal rings worn under it. Rings were worn on all fingers, often covering the whole length of the finger. The very old motive of a snake with a precious stone in its head was common. Wedding-rings especially were highly crafted and ornamented. Many rings were decorated with inlaid enamel instead of precious stones.

German book ornamentation

Johann Gutenberg worked on the construction of a printing press in Strassburg between 1436 and 1444, but it was not until 1459 that he began printing from movable type in Mainz, and Mainz is now considered to be the cradle of the art of printing in Europe.

German book ornamentation is as old as the art of printing. The Latin Psalter printed in Mainz by Fust and Schöffer contained 306 initials carved in wood and metal and printed in two colours. But two-colour printing was difficult at that time and in later editions blank spaces were left for the illuminator. In the 1570s other printers, too, began to decorate their books typographically with ornaments. In 1472 a Gothic alphabet of initials was published in Augsburg, at first used in Rempipollis' Guldin-Bible, then in Bishop Saloma's *Glossa* in Konstanz; the Augsburg Bibles of the 1580s also were often ornamented with initials carved in wood. But all these ornaments were Gothic and were only gradually superseded by Renaissance ornaments in the 16th century.

During the Renaissance Germany had a number of centres of book-ornamentation. First of all was Augsburg where printing was introduced in 1468 by Georg Leiner, whose books excelled in Gothic type and careful printing. The break with Gothic art came in Augsburg with Hans Burgkmair in 1508. He soon became the favourite artist of the Augsburg printing offices. Another important artist was the painter Daniel Hopfer, who from 1514 supplied Augsburg printers with drawings for ornaments and initials that show no Italian influence.

Erhard Ratdolt, who previously had worked in Venice, printed in Augsburg from 1486. Hans Othmar was the ancestor of a famous family of printers at the beginning of the 16th century; his son was of great service to book ornamentation and illustration. The technically most perfect of the books printed in Augsburg were those produced by Erhard Öglin, a contemporary of Hans Othmar's; Öglin was appointed the emperor's printer.

The first printer in Nuremberg, about 1470, was Johann Sensenschmid. In a short time several printers settled here and their books soon attained a world-wide reputation. But in Nuremberg book ornamentation was not of a high standard until Anton Skoberger printed his German Bible in 1483, using woodcuts used in a Bible printed in Cologne in 1480, bought there by Heinrich Quetell.

For a long time the initials in the books printed in Nuremberg retained the Gothic character, until Albrecht Dürer during his second Italian voyage in 1513 adopted the Renaissance. Especially remarkable among his designs are a large children's alphabet and two smaller ornamental alphabets. His pupil Hans Springinklee also produced excellent work. Dürer and Springinklee worked for three Nuremberg printing offices, those of Georg Stüchs, Hieronymus Hölzel and Pr. Peypus, who was the first Nuremberg printer to employ a roman type-face.

Basle was the centre of wood-block printing, which preceded printing from movable type. Brant's *Narrenschiff* (Ship of Fools) published in 1494 already shows the beginning of a development in book ornamentation on a realistic basis and in an artistic manner. In Basle, as in other printing centres, the conflict between Gothic and Renaissance art lasted for some time. The first book to be printed in Basle with Renaissance ornamentation was produced by Michel Furter in 1513. Hans Holbein, who worked in Basle in 1518, was instrumental to the development of Renaissance book ornamentation in Basle. His masterful blending of the figurative with the ornamental, his realistic representation of nature and his thorough knowledge of architecture soon set the fashion and printers deemed it an honour to publish his drawings. In the first half of the 16th century Basle was so famous for high standards of printing that the greatest contemporary scholars, including Erasmus of Rotterdam and Sir Thomas More, had their works printed in Basle. After Holbein's death book ornamentation declined in Basle.

The first printing office in Cologne was opened by Ulrich Zell in 1466. But here the transition from Gothic to Renaissance took a long time. Cologne had little contact with Italy, and consequently it was not until the 1620s that books with

Renaissance ornaments were printed in Cologne, and these ornaments were mostly copies of the Basle and Nuremberg schools.

Wittenberg owes its reputation as one of the most productive printing centres to Martin Luther and Lucas Cranach the elder. Georg Rhau became famous for printing Luther's and Melanchthon's prayer-books. The most important Wittenberg printer in the 16th century was Hans Lufft, who printed Luther's first Bible with illustrations by Lucas Cranach.

In the high and late Renaissance the great artists were displaced by craftsmen whose works despite their dexterity and thorough knowledge of the forms and tendencies of the Renaissance could not rival those of the early Renaissance.

BAROQUE

In contrast to the cool harmony of classicism and of the Renaissance, baroque art is spirited and dynamic. The forms of classical antiquity, the Renaissance and classicism appeal to the intellect but nevertheless satisfy in their elegance and balance as well as their graceful ornaments. Baroque art, however, cannot be approached intellectually; its principal aim is to surprise and overwhelm with powerful displays.

In the Renaissance, and to some extent in the northern late Gothic, the concept of achieving absolute harmony of all aspects of life replaced the medieval concept of life on earth as merely a stage to the all-important after-life. It was natural for Renaissance man to turn to antiquity which had a much more enlightened philosophy than the Middle Ages. After the Reformation the northern nations, especially the Calvinistic ones, continued the development of the Renaissance. In catholic countries, however, men again embraced the contemplation of an incomprehensible and inexplicable, and yet eternal, after-life. This produced heavy and oppressive art forms to which stirring, almost violent elements were added. In architecture, and especially in ornamentation, the clear profiles of the Renaissance were replaced by complex and ponderous forms.

Although in the beginning Baroque art was heavy and oppressive, in the second quarter of the 17th century the feeling of oppression was replaced by the sentiment of enchanted, excited enthusiasm, of indulging in a newly acquired world of feeling and art of supernatural greatness, vigour and liveliness.

Baroque art spread from Italy to Spain, southern and western Germany and Belgium, but met resistance in northern Europe. The contrast between catholic and aristocratic Belgium and Calvinist and middle-class Holland is personified by Rubens and Franz Hals. Later, under Louis XIV, Baroque also flourished in France.

Finally, northern Europe, especially England and northern Germany, adopted Baroque to a certain degree, as a consequence of the gradual change of Baroque from a purely ecclesiastic to a profane art. In northern Europe older traditions influenced and transformed the forms of the Italian Baroque. The Thirty Years' War in Germany and the threat of a Turkish invasion of Austria impeded an independent, homogenous development of Baroque in these countries. However, Germany recovered surprisingly quickly from the ravages of the Thirty Years' War.

Generally we can say that Austria and southern Germany were influenced by the Italian Baroque, and northern Germany by that of the Netherlands. Elements of the Renaissance, chiefly Tuscan columns, can still be seen in German architecture and furniture in the late 17th and even in the 18th century. Consequently we may assume a good deal of conservatism in German art, which is principally due to the conservatism of the craft guilds.

Boule furniture

This furniture has been famous and sought after for over 250 years. However, most of the examples are in museums or private collections. André Charles Boule was one of the leading cabinet-makers in France. One of the main reasons for his success, apart from his skill, was the great emphasis on luxury at that time. Furthermore, just as he began his career, a complete transformation in French furniture decoration occurred.

The furniture common in France until then was simple and rather crude, consisting mainly of chests and cupboards constructed from boards usually held together by projecting metal-clasps or brackets. In order to hide these, the furniture was often coated with oil paint or covered with painted linen. But already towards the end of the 14th century ornamentation of the larger pieces of furniture in imitation of architecture began to be developed. The use of grooves and dowels instead of metal brackets not only increased stability, but also produced a pleasant exterior. But for a long time, up to the 16th century, paint was still used to decorate furniture.

But Boule was not the originator of his particular style. Chests and cupboards in a similar style with inlaid ivory were already used in the 14th century. This furniture was mostly of oriental origin, and was decorated with quotations from the Koran surrounded by graceful arabesques. At this time marquetry was also used extensively in France, and furniture decorated with marquetry was imported from Spain, Italy, Flanders and India.

With the excessive luxury of the 17th century, furniture became so elaborately decorated that it ceased to be functional and became purely a showpiece, which is the only fault of Boule furniture.

André-Charles Boule was born in Paris in 1642. He was the son or grandson of the well known cabinet-maker Pierre Boule. It was a great distinction for Boule that at the early age of 29 he was appointed court cabinet-maker with a residence in the Louvre. The number of artists thus favoured was very small. There are no records to show whether he produced any furniture for the king before his move to the Louvre. His name first appears in the court records in 1669. His most beautiful piece of work while he was at court was a cabinet for the dauphin. The Boule furniture in the Louvre was soon, having been seriously damaged by dampness in the palace and being already a little out of fashion, transferred to the *garde mobilier* (furniture depository) rather than being restored.

In August 1720 a fire broke out in the carpenter Marteau's timber-yard, which spread so rapidly to Boule's workshops and house that only a few items of his extensive art collection could be saved. Apart from his very valuable stock of wood, Boule lost his collection of copper-engravings, drawings and antique statues; he assessed the damage at an astounding 208,570 livres.

Boule never became prosperous. He was pursued by creditors and had to abandon his residence in the Louvre in order to escape them. Actions were brought against him even by his workmen and customers. However, he was respected and admired for his work until his death in 1732.

He left four sons: Jean-Philippe, Pierre-Benoit, Charles-André and Charles-Joseph, who all became cabinet-makers. Two of them worked together with their father in the Louvre and occupied his house after his death. The other two established themselves outside the Louvre. Pierre-Benoit left the Louvre between 1720 and 1725 and established himself in Faubourg St. Antoine, but he seems to have lived in very straitened circumstances and he died without descendants. The most talented of the brothers was Charles-André, who, in order to avoid being mistaken for his brothers, called himself Boule de Sène, because he lived in Rue de Sèvres which was then spelled Sène.

Baroque faience in France

With the gradual decline of Renaissance ceramic art during the 17th century generally, ceramics in France also sank to the level of purely functional pottery for daily use. However, after Louis XIV's edict that all royal and state ceramic table ware was to be faience, ceramic art began to flower again in France. Duke Charles de Gonzaga in about 1600 brought the de Conrade family from Savona to Nevers, where it founded a ceramic workshop which remained in its possession for several generations. Other workshops were established by Barthélemy Bourcier, Nicolas Estienne and Pierre Custode.

Ceramic art in Nevers can be divided into five periods of decoration:
(1) Italian style, 1600–1660;
(2) Persian style, 1630–1700;
   Chinese and Japanese styles, 1600–1750;
   French style, 1640–1789;
(3) style of Rouen, 1700–1789;
   style of Moustiers, 1730–1789;
(4) wax style, 1770–1789;
(5) decadence, from 1789.

Nevers was especially famous for its statues of saints and paintings in a characteristic blue, as well as its imitations of Persian, Chinese and Japanese ceramics, which were succeeded by imitations of the faience of Rouen and Moustiers. The ceramic art of Nevers can therefore hardly be called original.

More important than Nevers was the ceramic manufacture of Rouen, where the workshops of the families Poterat, Guilliband and others raised the art to a flowering state in the middle of the 17th century. In its beginning Rouen faience resembled Italian and Dutch ceramics, but at the end of the 17th century an original style developed. This style (blue design on a white ground) reminds one of lace, embroidery, book ornaments or marquetry; it is principally an imitation of the drawings of Etienne de l'Aulue, Theodore de Bry, Virgilius Solis Beham and others. But following the fashion of the time, Persian and East Asiatic motives came into use, especially the motive of the horn of plenty. The addition of flowers, plants, rocaille-ornaments, birds and insects gradually deprived this style of its original character, but it maintained its symmetry.

In southern France the centres for faience were Moustiers and Marseille. The works from Moustiers were in the beginning blue on a white background; its later polychromatic works were of such high quality that they were imitated in Rouen and Nevers. The faience of Marseille was polychromatic from the beginning and had very delicate moulding.

Dutch faience

Dutch faience shows a distinct Japanese influence because of the trade connections between Holland and Japan in the 17th century. The Dutch East India Company, founded in 1602, had promoted trade with East Asia so successfully that in 1640 Japan expelled the Spanish and Portuguese traders and gave the Dutch the monopoly in trading with Europe.

The Dutch faience industry began with the formation of a guild in Delft in 1611. The most important members were Hendrick Gerritoz and Hermann Pietersz, who consequently can be considered the founders of this industry in Delft.

During the first 50 years the ornamentation of Delft faience was clumsy and over-ornate. The main motives were groups of figures framed with garlands, flowers, fruits, putti and horns of plenty with rather dark, mostly brown-violet outlines. Polychromy was used occasionally, but consisting chiefly only of yellow tones with red high-lights. Delft faience of that time much resembled that of Nevers. The work of Hendrick Goltsius in Harlem are a laudable exception. In 1650 the Delft faience industry began to develop rapidly and vigorously. Mediocre decorators gave way to excellent painters, and the craftsmen to experienced manufacturers. A sign of how weak a foundation this industry stood on before 1640 is the fact that from 1611 to 1640 only eight potters passed the examination for master, whereas between 1651 and 1660 more than 20 new masters were appointed. Delft faience became famous throughout the world and orders became so large that soon 26 manufactures had been established. The Delft faience industry was mainly promoted by Abraham de Kooge and Aelbregt de

Keizer; the latter was famous especially for his imitations of Japanese porcellain. De Kooge, on the other hand, tried to express the essence of faience with a milky tin-white glazing with firm outlines but soft half-tones, and he produced beautiful cameo-like tiles. F. V. Frytom also preferred a two-tone effect to polychromy and, principally in his landscapes, produced veritable masterpieces. The flowering of Dutch faience is no doubt closely connected with the flowering of Dutch painting as well as the success of Dutch overseas trade.

At the beginning of the 18th century Delft faience manufacture underwent a transformation. Until then faience had been expensive and within the reach of only wealthy people. Probably because of over-production, competition between manufacturers became very intense and forced prices down. Manufacturers adapted their products to the needs and taste of their new, less wealthy customers, and faience manufacture ceased to be an art and became a craft. Some artists tried to revive the earlier art of monochrome painting, for instance J. Verhaagen who produced his finest works between 1725 and 1735 but then was forced to turn to mass manufacture. At the same time Piet Vizeer managed to give his colours a splendour never achieved before. Dresden china was imitated with great success by Zacharia Dextra and J. P. Dextra, but these imitations lacked true artistic expression.

The decline of the Dutch faience industry was accelerated by the growing success of faience industries in other countries and by the spread of porcelain.

Beside Delft, faience was produced in Harlingen, Westraven near Utrecht, Utrecht, Arnsheim and Amsterdam.

ROCOCO

After the death of Louis XIV of France in 1715 a reaction set in against the excessive splendour and pomp of Versailles and the cermonial way of life. The centre of French life was transferred from Versailles back to Paris and new town houses were built which were smaller and more comfortable than the Baroque palaces.

Instead of pillars and pilasters panelling was used to decorate interior walls, and the whole range of colours became less pompous and lighter. Façades lost the pedantry of true classicism. This development accelerated rapidly under the Regency of the Duke of Orleans, and the new art was called *Stile Régence* (Regency) in France.

One of the most important painters was Gille-Marie Oppenort (1672–1742), a pupil of Mansart, Bernini and Pozzo, who displayed his genius in the decoration of the Palais Royal. Germain Boffrand (1667–1754) was instrumental in the dissimination of the new art abroad.

Other leading artists beside Oppenort were Claude Gillot (1673–1722), Claude Audran (1658–1739) and Jean Antoine Watteau (1684–1721). Remarkable for the genius of this epoch is the development of the 'singeries' (i.e. representations of apes) introduced by Gillot and further developed by Christophe Huet, who died in 1759. By far the most important painter of that period is Watteau, who produced admirable works of art, especially his chinoiseries, which, however, ethnographically have no relation with China, but in which people saw the realization of their dream of a land of merriment and grace.

The asymmetry manifested in Rococo is not the first example of it in the history of art; it had already appeared in Gothic art. The naturalism, caprice and exclusiveness in the subjects of the later Middle Ages induced an inclination to East Asiatic models. Consequently Rococo, too, necessarily inclined towards East Asiatic art.

In Germany the whole period of this art from Louis XIV until the advent of classicism is called Rococo, whilst in France its earliest period is called *Stile Régence* and its later period Rocaille or Louis XV style. Rocaille is derivated from the word 'roc' (rock or stone), stone- or shell-work used for adorning grottos, which was already frequently used in the Baroque.

Important artists of the Louis XV style were Juste Aurèle Meissonier, Thomas Germain, Jean Baptiste, Lecoux, René Michel Slodtz, the goldsmith Babel, Boucher, François de Cuvilliés, who was very influential in south and west Germany, and Jean Pillement.

In France Rococo was not dominated by the court, whereas in Germany it was a court-art. It is not surprising that Germany after the ravages of the Thirty Years' War tried to find support in the art of a neighbouring nation. After the Spanish war of succession some regions of the Austrian empire had looked to Italy more than to Germany; consequently in Austria, as well as in south-west Germany, the Italian influence is very marked, whilst in west and north Germany the French and Dutch influence predominates. But German Rococo can by no means be considered as a sort of degenerated French Rococo. In contrast with France, Germany has a true Rococo architecture, which developed independently from France, although influenced by Italy. There are even Rococo buildings in Germany which are older than Rococo ones in France. In France the exterior of Rococo buildings was very severe, whereas the German exteriors were exuberant and fanciful. German Rococo is Baroque art set free.

The new elements introduced to German Rococo are to be attributed to Habermann, Nilson and Meil, but many French artists, too, worked in Germany, especially Cuvillié. Frederick the Great also called many French artists to his court.

THE PLATES

Plate 1. Objects from the tombs at Ancona, Peru

Figs. 1, 5 and 14. Spindles of hardwood with clay cylinders. – Figs. 2, 4, 6 and 12. Scarves, also used as head-dress. – Fig. 3. Pearl necklace. – Figs. 7 and 9. Painted earthenware. – Figs. 8, 10 and 11. Pouches. – Fig. 13. Fragment of a painted earthenware vessel. (A. Stübel and W. Reiss, *Das Gräberfeld von Ancona.*)

Plate 2. Fabrics from the tombs at Ancona, Peru

Figs. 1–11. Cotton and wool fabrics and embroidery. (A. Stübel and W. Reiss, *Das Gräberfeld von Ancona*.)

1

2

4

3

5

7

6

9

8   11

10

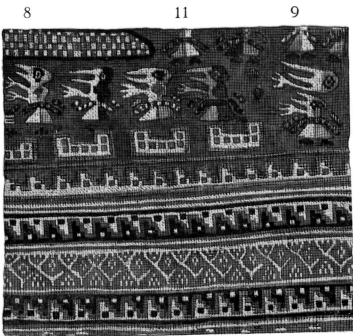

Plate 3. Polychromy in Egyptian architecture

Fig. 1. Capital with caulicles from the isle of Philae, 18th dynasty (Prisse d'Avennes, *Histoire de l'Art Égyptien*). – Fig. 2. Capital from the Dromos, 1st century BC (Max Baumgärtel, *Allgemeine Geschichte der bildenden Künste*). – Figs. 3 and 4. Decorations of mouldings (Prisse d'Avennes). – Fig. 5. Bundlepillar at Karnak, era of Touthmes III, 18th dynasty (Prisse d'Avennes). – Fig. 6. Pilaster from Thebes, 18th dynasty (Prisse d'Avennes.)

1

2

3

4

5

6

Plate 4. Egyptian ceiling and wall decoration

Figs. 1 and 3. Ceiling decoration from Memphis, 18th dynasty – Figs. 2, 4, 5, 6 and 12. Friezes of flowers from the necropolis of Thebes, 18th–20th dynasty. – Figs. 7 and 8. Friezes of flowers from tombs. – Fig. 9. Ceiling decoration from the necropolis of Thebes, 18th dynasty. – Fig. 10. Portrait of the Pharaoh Mienptah-Hotephimat, necropolis of Thebes, 19th dynasty. – Fig. 11. Ceiling decoration from the necropolis of Thebes, 20th dynasty. (Prisse d'Avennes, *Histoire de l'Art Égyptien.*)

Plate 5. Egyptian ornaments on wood

Figs. 1, 4, 6 and 8. Wooden pillars from Thebes, 18th and 20th dynasty. – Figs. 2, 3, 10 and 11. – Furniture from the necropolis of Thebes, 18th and 20th dynasty. – Figs. 5, 7 and 9. Utensils from various periods. (Prisse d'Avennes, *Histoire de l'Art Égyptien*.)

Plate 6. Egyptian fabrics and jewellery

Figs. 1, 3 and 23–25. Fabrics and embroideries (Prisse d'Avennes, *Histoire de l'Art Égyptien*). – Figs. 2, 13, 18 and 22. Fabrics (Fischbach, *Ornamente der Gewebe*). – Figs. 4–10, 12, 14–17, 19–21. Jewellery of various ages (Prisse d'Avennes). – Fig. 11. Fabric from the time of Amenophi II, 15th century BC (Anton Springer, *Handbuch der Kunstgeschichte*).

1 2 3

4 7 8 13

5 6 9 10

11 12

14 15 22

17 16

18 23 19 24 20 21 25

26

Plate 7. Egyptian ceramics

Fig. 1. Prisoner in bas-relief, faience, 20th dynasty, Gizeh Museum. – Fig. 2. Bowl, faience, 18th dynasty. – Fig. 3. Ring, faience, Ptolemaic period. – Fig. 4. Amulet, Middle Empire. – Fig. 5. Ushabti (sarcophagus), faience, height 195 mm, Gizeh Museum. – Fig. 6. Bowl, 19th dynasty, British Museum. – Fig. 7. Vase with cover, terra-cotta, 19th dynasty – Fig. 8. Cartouche of Amenhotep II, 18th dynasty. – Fig. 9. Amulet, faience, 25th dynasty. (Wallis, *Egyptian Ceramic Art.*)

1

2

3

4

5

6

7

8

9

Plate 8. Assyrian glazed tiles and frescos

Fig. 1. Fresco (Max Baumgärtel, *Allgemeine Geschichte der bildenden Künste*). – Fig. 2. Fresco in the palace of King Ashurnasirpal at Nimrud (Georges Perrot et Charles Chipiez, *Histoire de l'Art dans l'Antiquité*). – Fig. 3. Wall-decoration of glazed tiles at Nimrud (Perrot et Chipiez). – Figs. 4–6. Wall-decorations of glazed tiles from the wall of the harem at Khorsabad (Perrot et Chipiez). Fig. 7. Similiar decoration in the palace of king Ashurnasirpal at Nimrud (Perrot et Chipiez). Fig. 8. Ornament of glazed tiles from the threshold of the palace at Nineveh (Perrot et Chipiez).

1

2

3

4

5

6

7

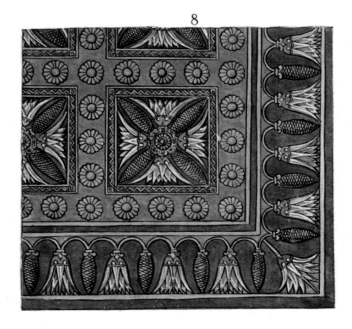

8

Plate 9. Phoenician glass and earthenware

Figs. 1, 2, 5 and 12. Glazed vessels from Camiro, Rhodes. – Figs. 3, 4, 8,10, 11, 13 and 14. Phoenician glass vessels, Crean collection. – Fig. 6. Cyprian vase, Eugène Piot collection. – Fig. 7. Bust from Cyprus, Louvre. Fig. 9. Phoenician necklaces, Louvre. (Georges Perrot et Charles Chipiez, *Histoire de l'Art dans l'Antiquité.*)

Plate 10. Persian glazed tiles

Fig. 1. Frieze of archers, glazed tiles, Susa. – Fig. 2. Frieze of lions, glazed tiles, Susa. (Georges Perrot et Charles Chipiez, *Histoire de l'Art dans l'Antiquité.*)

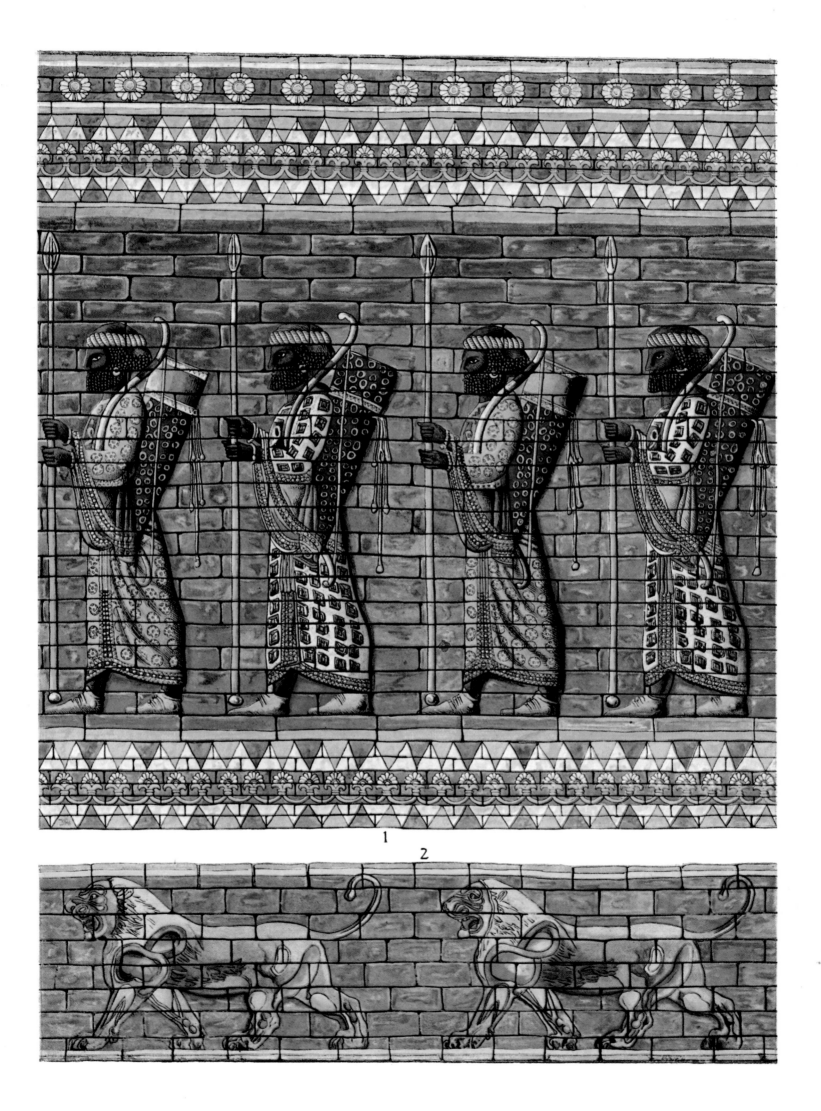

1

2

Plate 11. Cretan ceramic art

Figs. 1, 3, 4 and 9. Vessels from the Kamares period (*Journal of Hellenic Studies*). – Figs. 2, 5, 6 and 8. Vessels in late Minoic style (Boyd-Hawes, *Gurnia*). – Figs. 7 and 10. Middle Minoic vessels from Phaestos (*Monumenti antichi*).

Plate 12. Mycenaean frescos

Fig. 1. Reconstruction of a figure of a frieze in the later palace of Tiryns. – Fig. 2. Reconstruction of a group of chariots in the same palace. – Fig. 3. Frieze of shields in the earlier palace of Tiryns. – Fig. 4. Frieze of spirals in the same palace. (Kaiserliches deutsches Archäologisches Institut in Athen, *Tiryns,* edited by Gerhardt Rodenwaldt, Rudolf Haekel and Noel Haton.)

1

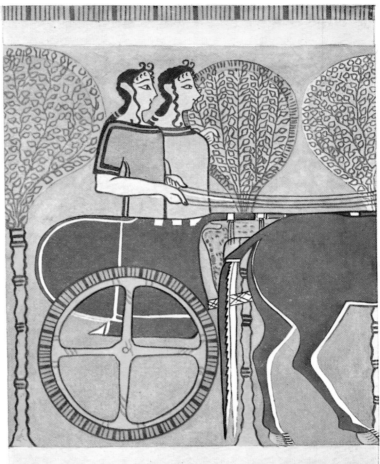

2

3

4

Plate 13. Greek decorated marble

Fig. 1. Cyma of the Phigalia temple (Fenger, *Die dorische Polychromie*). – Fig. 2. Antefix from the Parthenon at Athens (Fenger). – Fig. 3. Cyma of the Propylaea at Athens (Fenger). – Figs. 4 and 5. Painted egg-mouldings from the Acropolis at Athens (Hittorf, *Restitution du temple d'Empédocle*). – Fig. 6. Painted moulding from the Acropolis at Athens (Hittorf). – Fig. 7. Torus from the Erechtheum at Athens (Hittorf). – Fig. 8. Female torso from the Acropolis at Athens (Hittorf). – Fig. 9. Cyma of the Tholi at Epidaurus. – Fig. 10. Antefix from Phiglia (Fenger). Fig. 11. Capital from the temple of Themis at Rhamnus (Fenger). – Fig. 12. Capital from the Parthenon at Athens. – Figs. 13, 14 and 15. Details of the drapery in Fig. 8.

Plate 14. Polychromy in Greek architecture

Fig. 1. Capital from the temple of Hera at Selinunt (Fenger, *Die dorische Polychromie*). – Fig. 2. Capital from the temple of Nike-Apteros at Athens (Fenger). – Fig. 3. Capital from the Propylaea at Athens (Fenger). – Fig. 4. Metope of clay, found at Phallazalle (Hittorf et Zanth, *Architecture antique de la Sicile ou receuil des plus intéressantes monuments d'architecture des villes et des lieux les plus remarquables de la Sicile ancienne*). Figs. 5 and 6. Mouldings from the temples of the Acropolis at Selinunt (Hittorf et Zanth). – Fig. 7. Coffer of the ceiling of the Erechtheum at Athens (von Quast, *Das Erechtheion zu Athen*). Fig. 8. Coffer of the ceiling of the Erechtheum at Athens (Durm, *Die Baukunst der Griechen*).

1   2   3

4   5   6

7   8

Plate 15. Types of Greek vases

Fig. 1. Rhyton (drinking vessel) in form of a deer's head, with cup, late vase-painting. – Fig. 2. Vessel in form of a woman's head. – Fig. 3. Apulian censer, combination of various styles. – Fig. 4. Apulian two-handled cup. Fig. 5. Hydria or Kalpis. – Fig. 6. Lekythos (vessel to hold consecrated oil), developed Attic style. – Fig. 7. Jug with Asiatic influences. – Fig. 8 and 9. Bowls with handles, later period. – Fig. 10. Crater (bowl for mixing wine with water). – Fig. 11. Amphora. – Fig. 12. Lekythos, combination of the black-figured, red-figured and polychromic styles. (Lau, *Die griechischen Vasen.*)

Plate 16. Greek marble mosaics

Fig. 1. Marble floor from Olympia (Poppe, *Sammlung von Ornamenten u. Fragmenten antiker Architektur, Skulptur, Mosaik and Toreutik*). – Figs. 2, 10 and 11. Marble mosaics (floors) from Eleusis (Poppe). – Figs. 3–9. Fragments of floors from Sicily, partly in the Museum of the Court of Biscari (Hittorf, *Restitution du temple d'Empédocle*).

1

2

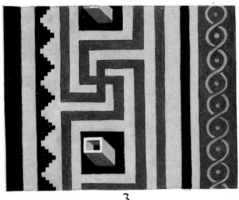

3

4

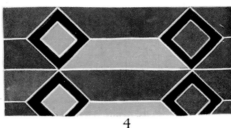

6

5

7

10

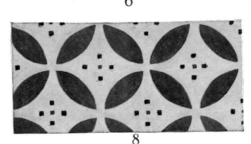

8

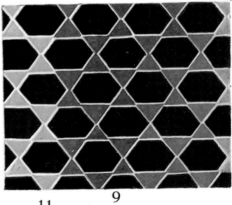

9

11

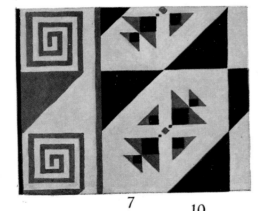

Plate 17. Etruscan frescos

Figs. 1, 3, 4 and 5. Painted clay tiles from Cervetri (Martha, *L'Art Etrusque*). – Figs. 2 and 8. Frescos from the tombs of Corneto-Tarquinia, 6th century BC (*Antike Denkmäler*). – Figs. 6 and 7. Painted sarcophagus of clay of the family of the Seianti, found near Chiusi (Poggio Cantarello).

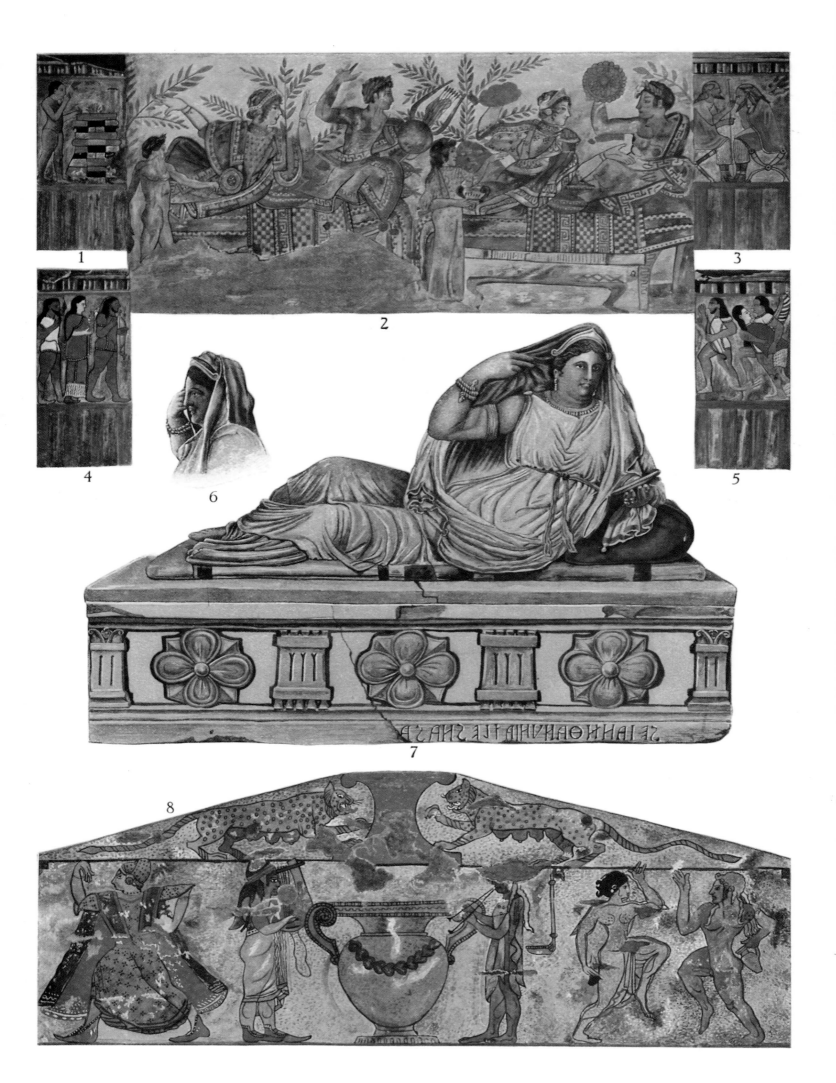

Plate 18. Wall-decorations from the Imperial Palace on the Palatine Hill

(Schwechten, *Wanddekorationen aus den Kaiserpalästen auf dem Palatin in Rom.*)

Plate 19. Roman marble mosaics

Fig. 1. Floor of a house in Brescia (Gruner, *Specimens of ornamental art*). – Fig. 2. Floor of a Roman villa near Wiltingen. – Figs. 3 and 4. Floor of a bath in a Roman villa near Vilbel (Frankfurt/Main). – Fig. 5. Floor of a Roman house in Trier. – Fig. 6. Head of a swordsman in the floor of a Roman villa in Nennig. – Fig. 7. Floor of a Roman villa in Euren (Vorlagensammlung der Kgl. Kungstgewerbebibiothek in Dresden).

Plate 20. Roman gold and enamel jewellery

Figs. 1, 3, 5–13, 17 and 20–23. Roman pins for garments, gold and enamel, Wiesbaden Museum (v. Cohausen, *Römischer Schmelzschmuck*). – Figs. 2, 4, 14 and 16. Roman earrings from Pompeii (Nicolini, *Pompeji*). – Figs. 15 and 24. Roman bracelets from Pompeii (Nicolini). – Figs. 18 and 19. Roman ring from Pompeii (Nicolini).

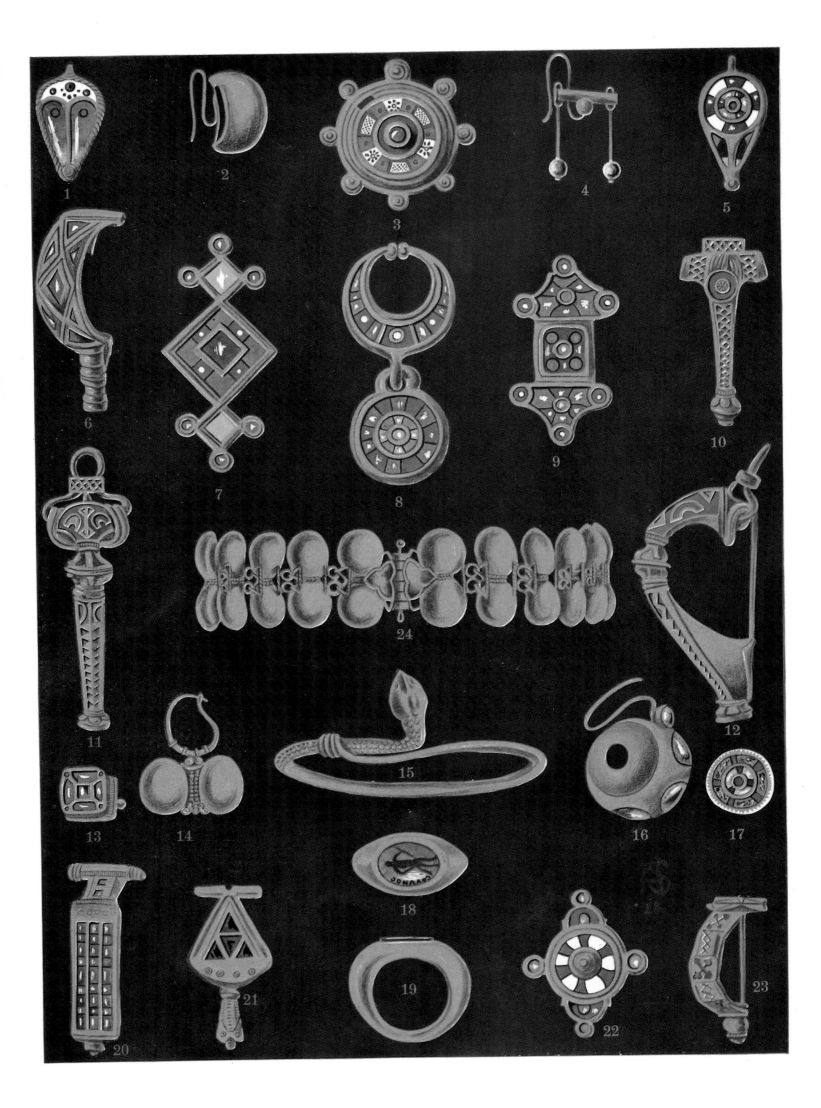

Plate 21. Pompeian frescos

Fig. 1. Fresco from the first period (Presuhn, *Die pompejanischen Wanddekorationen*). – Fig. 2. Fresco from the second period (Nicolini, *Pompeji*).

1   2

Plate 22. Pompeian frescos

Figs. 1, 2. Frescos in the House of the Labyrinth, second period. (Gruner, *Specimens of ornamental art.*)

1 2

Plate 23. Pompeian frescos

Fig. 1. Fresco from the third period. – Fig. 2. Fresco from the fourth period. (Nicolini, *Pompeji*.)

1   2

Plate 24. Roman-Hellenistic frescos

Fig. 1. Fresco from Herculaneum (Zahn, *Ornamente*). Fig. 2. Fresco from Pompeii (Nicolini, *Pompeji*).

1

2

Plate 25. Roman-Hellenistic wall decoration

Fig. 1. Frieze from Herculaneum (Zahn, *Ornamente*). – Figs. 2–4. Friezes from Pompeii (Zahn). – Fig. 5. Fountain in a niche in the House of Medusa at Pompeii (Gruner, *Specimens of ornamental art*).

Plate 26. Pompeian Painted stucco

Figs. 1, 6, 7, 8 and 13. Painted columns and capitals of stone, covered with stucco. – Figs. 2–5 and 9–12. Painted interior mouldings. (Zahn, *Ornamente aller klassischen Kunstepochen*.)

Plate 27. Roman marble mosaics

Figs. 1–4, 7, 10 and 11. Marble mosaics from Pompeii. – Figs. 5, 6, 8 and 9. Rosettes of marble and vitreous paste from Herculaneum (Zahn, *Ornamente*).

Plate 28. Pompeian furniture

Fig. 1. Bronze chest. – Figs. 2–5. Bedstead of wood and bronze. (Nicolini, *Pompeji.*)

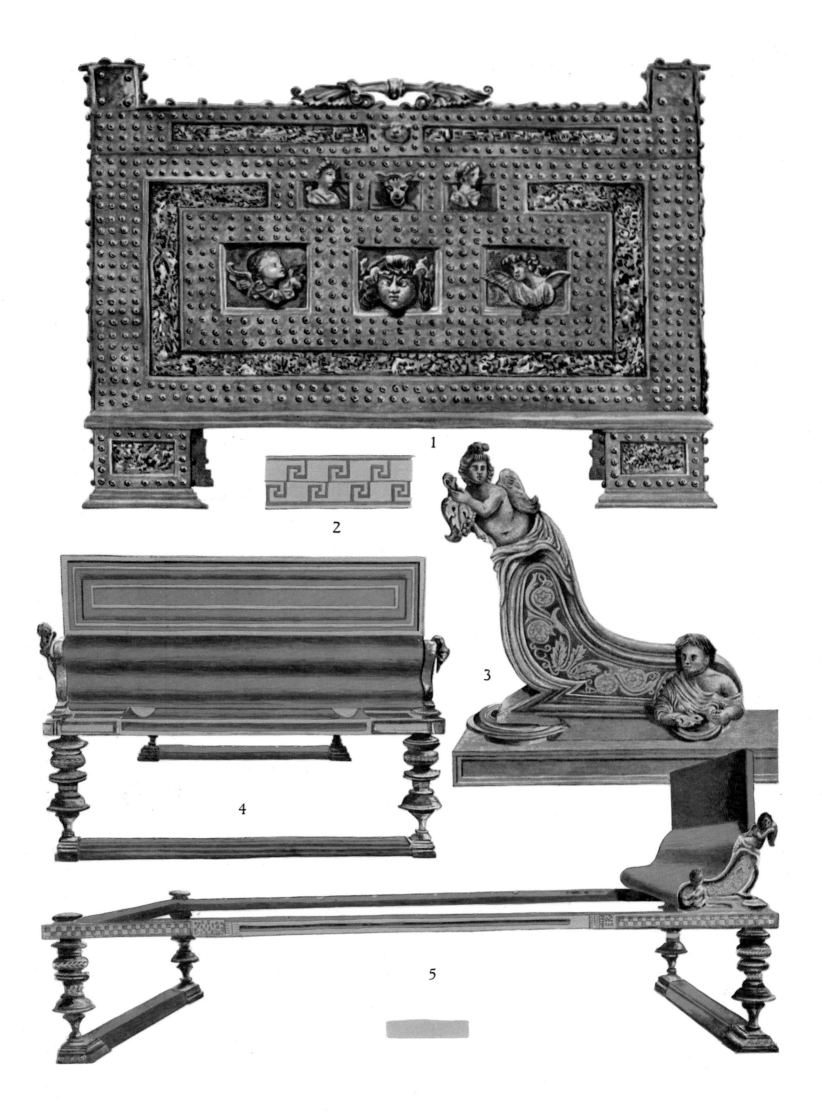

Plate 29. Roman-Hellenistic glass vessels

Figs. 1–7 and 9–13. Glass vessels found at Pompeii. – Fig. 8. Funeral urn of blue glass with a coating of white glass and bas-reliefs, found at Pompeii. (Nicolini, *Pompeji.*)

1

2

3

4

5

6

7

8

9

10

11

12

13

Plate 30. Paintings in the Buddhist cave-temples of Ajantâ, 6th century AD

Figs. 1–3, 7 and 10. Paintings in coffers of rock ceilings. – Fig. 4. Portrait of Buddha. – Figs. 5, 6, 8 and 9. Painted rock pillars. (Griffith, *Paintings in the Buddhist cave-temples of Ajantâ, Kandeh in India.*)

Plate 31. Ceiling decoration in the Buddhist cave-temples of Ajantâ

Figs. 1, 2, 4 and 5. Paintings on smooth rock-ceilings. – Fig. 3. Painting on a coffer of a rock ceiling. (Griffith, *Paintings in the Buddhist cave-temples of Ajantâ, Kandeh in India*).

1

2

3

4

5

Plate 32. Coptic fabrics

Fig. 1. Silk edging, Abrabic influence, 7th century (P. Forrer, *Römische und Byzantinische Seidentextilien aus dem Gräberfelde von Achmim-Panopolis*). – Fig. 2. Silk edging of a gobelin with animals, 7th century (Forrer). – Fig. 3. Christ as teacher, from a series of pictures representing the life of Christ from a pallium pontificium, 6th century (Forrer). – Fig. 4. Silk edging, 6th century (Forrer). – Fig. 5. Silk material with Cufic letters, 7th century (Forrer). – Fig. 6. Silk material with the Holy Virgin, the infant Jesus and a worshipper in front of a house, 6th century. – Fig. 7. Christ at the cross, from the same pallium as in fig. 3 (Forrer). – Fig. 8. The Angel of the Annunciation, from the same pallium (Forrer). – Figs. 9 and 11. Silk materials found in a tomb at Antinoë, Upper Egypt, 5th century (Lessing, *Gewebesammlung des Kgl. Kunstgewerbemuseums in Berlin*). Fig. 10. Silk edging with the monogram of Christ, 7th century (Forrer).

Plate 33. Persian fabrics from the era of the Sassanid dynasty

Figs. 1 and 2. Fabrics in the Church of Servatius in Maëstricht, 3rd–7th century (Fischbach, *Die wichtigsten Webeornamente*). – Fig. 3. Fabric with the four-bodied sealion representing the four seasons, from Görz (Fischbach). – Fig. 4. Fabric in St. Ursula's, Cologne (Fischbach). – Fig. 5. Bowl of the treasure of St. Denis, said to have belonged to King Chosru I of Persia (531–579 AD), whose portrait is in the centre of the bowl; probably part of the gifts of Haroun-al-Rashid to Charlemagne. – Fig. 6. Silk material, Berlin Museum of Applied Arts, 6th or 7th century (Lessing). – Fig. 7. Fabric from the era of King Chosru II (591–628 AD), probably manufactured at Ctesiphon, now in St. Ursula's, Cologne (Lessing).

1   2

3   4

5

6   7

Plate 34. The treasure of Petrosa

Fig. 1. Octagonal bowl. – Figs. 2 and 5. Brooches. – Figs. 3, 4 and 6. Twelve-sided bowl (Fig. 3: side-view, Fig. 4: handle seen from above). (Linas, *Les origines de l'orfèvrerie cloisonnée.*)

Plate 35. Merovingian goldsmiths' work

Figs. 1 and 2. Clasp in the Museum at Cluny, Paris (Linas, *Les origines de l'orfèvrerie cloisonnée*). – Figs. 3 and 4. Reliquary in the Monastery St. Maurice (Linas). – Fig. 5. Sword cross-guard (Linas). – Figs. 6, 7, 11 and 13. Gold brooches made by the Burgundians Undhio and Ello (Linas). – Fig. 8. Gold cup, belonging to 10 and 12. – Fig. 9. Silver brooches (Havard, *Histoire de l'orfèvrerie française).* – Figs. 10 and 12. Gold dish (Linas). – Fig. 14. Lock of a purse (Linas). – Fig. 15. Sword hilt from Childerich's grave (Linas). – Fig. 16. Buckle of a belt (Linas). – Fig. 17. Ear-ring (Linas).

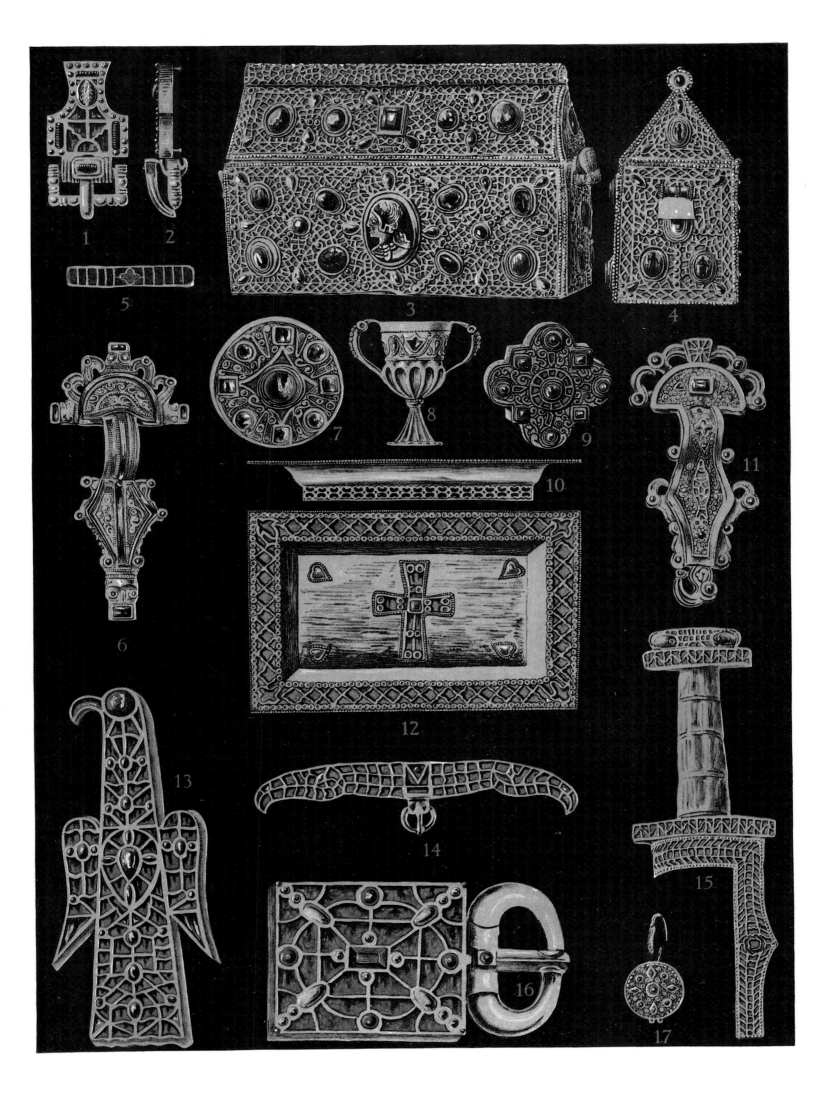

Plate 36. The treasure of Guarrazar

Fig. 1. Votive crown of the Abbot Theodosius in Guarrazar. – Fig. 2. Suspender for a votive crown. – Fig. 3. Cross for a procession, called de la Victoria, in the Holy Chamber of Oviedo Cathedral, 9th century. – Fig. 4. Votive crown of King Receswint (King of Spain 649–672) in Guarrazar. – Fig. 5. Cross for a procession, called de los Angeles, in the Holy Chamber of Oviedo Cathedral, 10th century. – Fig. 6. Votive crown. – Figs. 7 and 9. Votive crosses. – Fig. 8. Reverse of the cross in Fig. 4. *(Monumentos de España.)*

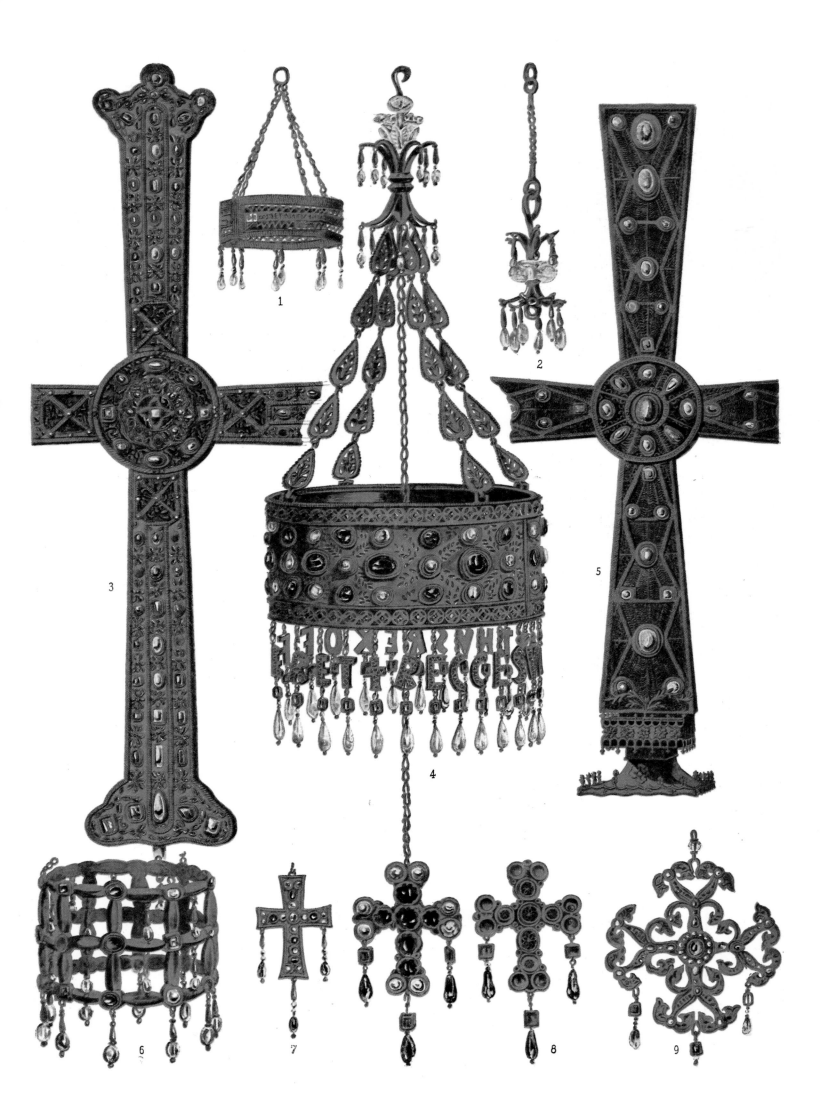

Plate 37. Early Byzantine interior decoration

Fig. 1. Interior of the baptestry of Ravenna Cathedral, San Giovanni in Fonte. Built by Archbishop Neo in 425–430, it is one of the most important monuments of polychrome art in the first centuries of Christianity, showing distinctly reminiscences of Roman tradition of art. The multi-colour marble decoration of the lower section of the walls is only partly preserved. The cupola is completely covered with mosaics. (Köhler, *Polychrome Meisterwerke der monumentalen Kunst in Italien.*)

Plate 38. Byzantine marble floor-mosaics

Figs. 1–7 and 12. Marble floors in St. Mark's in Venice (Hessemer, *Arabische und altchristliche Bauverzierungen*). Figs. 8–11 and 13–15. Marble floors in St. Sophia's in Constantinople (Salzenberg, *Altchristliche Baudenkmale in Konstantinopel*).

Plate 39. Early Byzantine glass-mosaics

Figs. 1–6 and 8–14. Mosaics from St. Lorenzo's, St. Clemente's, etc., 5th and 6th century (Lacroix et Seré, *Le moyen âge et la renaissance). –* Fig. 7. Mosaic from St. Prisa's near Capua (Salazaro, *Monumenti della Italia meridionale).*

Plate 40. Byzantine glass-mosaics

Fig. 1: Glass-mosaic frieze from Galla Placidra's church of entombment in Ravenna (von Quast, *Die altchristlichen Bauwerke von Ravenna.*) – Figs. 2–11. Glass-mosaic from St. Mark's, Venice (Hessemer, *Arabische und altitalienische Bauverzierungen*).

Plate 41. Byzantine enamel

Figs. 1 and 2. Cover of a book from the library of St. Mark's, Venice (Pasini, *Il tresoro di St. Marco*). – Fig. 3. Dish from the treasury of St. Mark's, Venice (Pasini). – Figs. 4, 6 and 7. Enamel fragments from St. Ambrosius' altar in Milan (Kondakow, *History of the monuments of Byzantine enamel,* collection A. W. Swenigorodskoi). – Fig. 5. Fragment of the dress of an image of the Holy Virgin (Kondakow).

Plate 42. Byzantine miniature painting

Figs. 1 and 8. From a 13th-century manuscript (Gagarin, *Collection of ancient Byzantine and Russian ornaments*). – Figs, 2, 4, 6, 10 and 12. From 12th-century manuscripts in the Bibliothèque Nationale, Paris. – Fig. 3. From an 11th-century Greek manuscript in St. Mark's Library, Venice. – Fig. 5. From a 10th-century manuscript (Gagarin). – Figs. 7 and 11. Initials from the *Breviorium Cassinense* in the Mazarin Library, Paris (Petzendorfer, *Schriftenatlas*). – Fig. 9. From a 6th-century manuscript in the Library at Turin. – Fig. 13. From a manuscript in the Bibliothèque Nationale, Paris.

Plate 43. Byzantine fabrics

Figs. 1–3, 6, 7, 9 and 10. Byzantine silk fabrics (Fischbach, *Ornamente der Gewebe*). Fig. 4. Drapery in the treasury of Aachen Cathedral and in the Louvre, Paris (Cahier et Martin, *Mélanges d'archéologie*). – Fig. 5. Drapery from St. Madelbertha's reliquary in Liège Cathedral, 10th century (Lessing, *Gewebesammlung des Kgl. Kunstgewerbemuseums in Berlin*). – Fig. 8. Drapery from Charlemagne's reliquary in Aachen (Cahier et Martin).

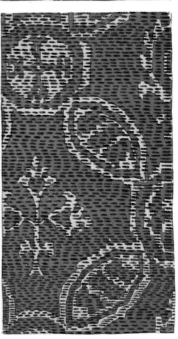

Plate 44. Russian miniature painting

Figs. 1, 8, 10, 12–18. Paintings from the 11th century. – Figs. 2–4 and 6. Paintings from the 12th century. – Figs. 7, 9, 11, 19 and 20. Paintings from the 15th century. (Butovsky, *Histoire de l'ornement russe.*)

Plate 45. Celtic miniature painting

Figs. 1–4, 7, 12 and 15. Head-pieces and borders from the 7th century in a gospel-book of Durrow in Trinity College, Dublin. – Figs. 5, 10, 11 and 14. Border from *The Royal Psamist,* 8th century. – Figs. 6, 8 and 9. From a painted page of the Latin Bible in the Monastery Library, St. Gallen, 9th century. – Fig. 13. Page from the Arundel Psalter, psalm 101, 11th century, British Museum. (M. D. Wyatt, *The art of illuminating.*)

NE EAVDI
ORATIONEM
MEA : ET CLA
MOR MS AD
EVENIAT

Plate 46. Celtic miniature painting

Figs. 1, 3 and 8. From St. Augustine's Psalter, 7th century, British Museum. – Fig. 2. From King David's psalms in St. John's College, Cambridge, 9th century. – Fig. 4. Beginning of St. Matthews's gospel, St. Petersburg gospel-book, 8th century. – Fig. 5. Initial at the beginning of a 10th-century psalter, British Museum. – Figs. 6 and 7. From St. Matthew's and St. John's gospels in the Public Library, Cambridge.

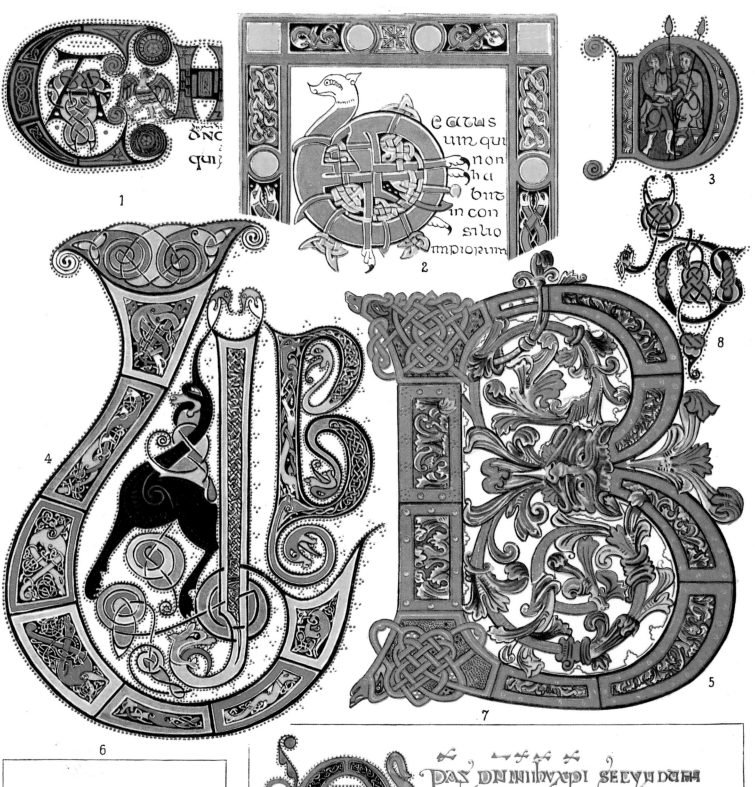

1

2

3

4

6

7

8

5

hanc lui
zemilia
SVFRA
noune
UNIteas
trinieas . Supruaza

PAX DN INIIHV XPI SECVNDVM
MATHE VM
FACTVM EST

CUM CONSUMMESSET IHS
sermones hos omnes DIXIT discipu

Plate 47. Italian Romanesque frescos

Fig. 1. Painting from the sanctuary of St. Angelo's Basilica, Formis. – Figs. 2–5. Paintings from the subterranean Church of St. Clemente, Rome. (Salazaro, *Monumenti della Italia meridionale.*)

Plate 48. Italian Romanesque miniature painting

Figs. 1, 3, 7, 8 and 12. Latin initials from the 12th century. – Fig. 2. Langobardian initial from the 11th century. – Figs. 4, 5, 6 and 9. Latin initials from the 11th century. – Figs. 10, 11, 14, 15 and 16. Langobardian initials from the 13th century. – Fig. 13. Latin initial from the 9th century. (*Paleographia artistica di Monte Cassino.*)

IG
NA
CV
LO:

Plate 49. Saracenic-Norman painting

Figs. 1, 3, 10 and 11. Fragments of the ceiling-paintings in the aisles of Capella Palatina, Palermo (Kutschmann, *Meisterwerke sarazenisch-normannischer Kunst in Sizilien und Unteritalien*). – Figs. 2, 5 and 6. Ceiling-painting in the central aisle of St. Pietro's Chapel, Palermo (Terzi, *La capella di San Pietro en Palermo*). – Fig. 4. Painted coffer of the ceiling of the lower choir (Kutschmann). – Figs. 7–9. Painting on the ceiling of a hall in the palace of Manfred of Chiaramonte, Palermo (Gailhaband, *L'architecture du Ve au XVIIe siècle*).

Plate 50. Saracenic-Norman silk

Fig. 1. Silk drapery from the 13th century. – Fig. 2. Silk drapery from the 11th century, Vienna Museum. – Figs. 3 and 6. Silk weaving from the 13th century, probably Lucresian imitation of Saracenic fabrics, Vienna, Halberstadt museums respectively. – Fig. 4. Silk drapery from the 13th century, Vienna – Fig. 5. Silk drapery from the 11th century. – Figs. 7 and 8. Silk weaving from the 13th century; the motive of Fig. 7 appears as a painting on a pillar in St. Bravo's, Harlem. – Fig. 9. 12th-century drapery from Palermo. (Fischbach, *Ornamente der Gewebe.*)

Plate 51. German Romanesque enamel

Figs. 1, 3 and 5–7. From St. Ursula's shrine, Cologne, made by Friedericus in 1170. – Figs. 2, 4, 8–12, 14 and 15. From St. Maurinus' shrine, Cologne, made by Friedericus in 1180. – Fig. 13. Plate from the ancient altar of Remartus at Stablo, made by Godefroid de Claire in 1150, Museum of Sigmaringen. – Figs. 16–21. From St. Albinus' shrine, Cologne, 1186. – Figs. 22–25. Decoration on a pillar in St. Anno's shrine, Siegburg, made in Cologne about 1183. (Falke und Frauberger, *Deutsche Schmelzarbeiten des Mittelalters und andre Kunstwerke der Kunsthistorischen Austellung zu Düsseldorf 1902–1904.*)

Plate 52. German Romanesque glass-painting

Fig. 1. From a window of the city parish church, Steyr, Austria, 1300. – Fig. 2. Rose from Strassburg Cathedral, end of the 13th century. – Fig. 3. From a window in the centre nave of Strassburg Cathedral, 1300. – Fig. 4. Window from the collegiate church, Wimpfen in Thuringia, 13th century, Darmstadt Museum. – Fig. 5. From Strassburg Cathedral, end of the 13th century. – Figs. 6 and 8. Window from St. Elizabeth's, Marburg, end of the 13th century. – Fig. 7. Window from St. Cunibert's, Cologne, 13th century. – Figs. 9–11. From St. Cunibert's, Cologne, 13th century.

Plate 53. German Romanesque ceilings and murals

Fig. 1. Soffit from the choir in St. Peter's, Schleswig, end of the 13th century. – Figs. 2 and 5. Border of an altar niche in Liebfrauenkirche, Halberstadt, end-13th century. – Fig. 3. Frieze from the choir in Braunschweig Cathedral, mid-13th century. – Fig. 4. Painting from the Long House of St. Severus', Boppard, 1230. – Figs. 6, 7 and 15. Painting from the window niches of St. Catherine's Chapel of Castel Hocheppau, 1140. – Fig. 8. Painting from St. Nicolaus', Windischmatrei, Austria, 13th century. – Fig. 9. Picture in the Karner's Rotunda, Hartberg, Austria, 13th century. – Figs. 10 and 11. Picture on the ceiling of St. Maria zur Höhe, Soest, beginning of the 13th century. – Fig. 12. Ceiling picture in St. Michael's, Hildesheim, 13th century. – Fig. 13. Picture from the choir in Braunschweig Cathedral, mid-13th century. – Figs. 14 and 16. Pictures from the choir of the nuns in the monastery of Gurk, Austria, mid-13th century. (Borrmann, *Aufnahmen mittelalterlicher Wand- und Deckenmalereien in Deutschland.*)

1. 2. 4. 5. 6. 7.

8. 9. 10. 11.

12. 13. 16. 14. 15.

Plate 54. German Romanesque miniature painting

Figs. 1, 5, 12 and 14. Initials from manuscripts from the 11th century (Wilding, *Bücherornamentik*). – Figs. 6–9 and 11. From the manuscript *Josephus, Antiquitates judaicae* from the 12th century in the Royal Library, Stuttgart (Petzendorfer, *Schriftenatlas*). – Fig. 10. From a manuscript from the 11th century (Lacroix et Seré, *Le moyen âge et la renaissance.*)

Plate 55. Scandinavian medieval tapestry

Figs. 1, 2 and 3. Cushion covers in the museum of Christiania (H. Grosch, *Altnor-wegische Teppichmuster*). – Fig. 4. Carpet from the church in Hedemarken, 11th century (Grosch). – Figs. 5 and 6. Carpets from the 11th century (Lacroix et Seré, *Le moyen âge et la renaissance.*)

1. 2.

3.

4.

5.

6.

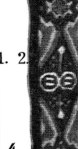

Plate 56. Spanish miniature painting

Figs. 1, 3–7. Initials from the Codex of the National Library, Madrid. – Fig. 2. The symbolical cross generally used in the early Middle Ages containing a and w and the four Evangelists according to the book *In Apokalypsiu* by Beato in Liébana towards the end of the 8th century, copied by the monk Albino in St. Millan de la Cogulla in 1178. (*Monumentos de España.*)

Plate 57. Spanish medieval glass-painting

Fig. 1. Window from the nave in Toledo Cathedral. – Figs. 2 and 3. Fragments of glass-pictures from St. Juan de los Reyes' Monastery. (*Monumentos de España.*)

1

2

3

Plate 58. French Romanesque mural painting

Figs. 1 and 6. Painted soffit of an arc in Cadonin Abbey (Dordogne), 13th century. – Figs. 2, 7 and 8. Pictures from St. Crépin's, Evron (Mayenne), 13th century. – Figs. 3–5. Norman paintings from the chapter-house, Séez Cathedral (Orne), 13th century. – Fig. 9. Cross of a rosette from the church of Pritz near Laval (Mayenne), 13th century. – Fig 10. Cross of a rosette from Cadonin Abbey (Dordogne), 13th century. – Figs. 11 and 12. Capitals from the church of Chateloi (Allier), 12th century. – Fig 13. Cross of a rosette from St. Géneri's (Orne), 13th century. – Figs. 14 and 18. Soffits from Chateau de Coucy (Aisne), 13th century. – Figs. 15, 16 and 17. Norman capitals from the church of St. Georges de Boscherville, 13th century. – Figs. 19, 21 and 23. Soffits from the church of St. Quiriau in Provins, 12th century – Fig. 20. Soffit from the church of St. Ours in Loches (Indre et Loire), 13th century. – Fig. 22. Picture on a wooden door-panel in Bayeux Cathedral, 13th century. – Figs. 24 and 25. Friezes from the church of St. Michel d'Aiguilhe near Puy (Haute-Loire), 13th century. (Gélis-Didot et Saffillée, *La peinture décorative en France du XIe siêcle.*)

Plate 59. French Gothic mural painting

Fig. 1: Soffit of an arc in the church of Villeneuve-les-Avignons (Gard), 14th century (Gélis-Didot et Saffillée, *La peinture décorative en France du XIe au XVIe siècle*). – Figs. 2 and 10. Rosette and groin of a vault from the church of Cusault (Maine et Loire), 13th century (Gélis-Didot). – Fig. 3. Wooden coffer of a ceiling in the church of Baillon-sur-Loire, 14th century (Gélis-Didot). – Fig. 4. Painted sculptures from the chapel of St. François-Xavier in Notre Dame de Paris (*Peintures murales des chapelles de Notre Dame de Paris*). – Fig. 5. Picture from Clermont Cathedral (Puy-de-Dôme) (Gélis-Didot). – Fig. 6: Painted sculptures from the chapel of St. Clothilde in Notre Dame de Paris (*Peintures murales.*) – Figs. 7 and 11. Painted sculptures in Rheims Cathedral (Gailhaband, *L'architecture au Ve au XVIIe siécle*). – Fig. 8. Soffit of a window in the church of St. Julien de Brionde (Haute-Loire), 14th century. – Fig. 9. Painted groin and rosette of a vault from Auxerre Cathedral, 13th century.

Plate 60. French floor-tiles

Fig. 1. From the castle of Margaret of Burgundy in Tonnerre (Yonne), 13th century. – Fig. 2. From the gallery of Notre Dame de l'Épine (Marne), 15th century. – Figs. 3 and 4. From the chapel of the monastery of Bretenil (Oise), 14th century. – Fig. 5. From Chancellor Rollin's town house in Dijon, 15th century. – Fig. 7. From the old hall of Touey (Yonne), 14th century. – Figs. 9, 13, 14, 16 and 17. From the church of St. Colombe's monastery (Yonne), 12th century. – Figs. 10–12 and 18–20. From the hall in the chapter-house of the cathedral of Cotanus (Manche), 13th century. – Fig. 15. Engraved stone tile from the altar of the Holy Virgin in the church of St. Denis (Seine), 13th century. – Fig. 21. From the church of Nivoin (Sauthe), 13th century. – Fig. 22. From the museum in Auxerre (Yonne), 14th century. – Fig. 23. From St. Michel's chapel in the college of St. Quentin (Aisne), 12th century. – Fig. 24. From the church of Nimelles (Yonne), 14th century. – Fig. 25. From the manor house of Sacy (Yonne), 14th century. – Fig. 26. From the castle of the Abbey of Vezelay (Yonne), 13th century. – Fig. 27. From the castle of Haulsy (Marne), 13th century. (Amé, *Les carrelages émaillés du moyen àge et de la renaissance.*)

Plate 61. French 13th-century glass-painting

Figs. 1 and 5. Le Mans Cathedral (Lacroix et Serré, *Le moyen age et la renaissance*). – Figs. 2, 4, 8, 9, 12 and 13. Chartres Cathedral (Cahier et Martin, *Mélanges d'archéologie*). – Fig. 3. Grisaille from St. Thoma's Cathedral in Bourges (Lacroix et Serré). – Figs. 6 and 10. Window of Bourges Cathedral (Lacroix et Seré). – Figs. 11 and 14. Painting from Le Mans Cathedral (Lacroix et Seré).

Plate 62. English medieval miniature painting

Figs. 1 and 5. From the 13th century. – Figs. 2, 3, 6 and 7. From the 14th century. – Fig. 4. From the 11th century. (Westwood, *Facsimiles of miniatures.*)

Plate 63. English medieval glass-painting

Fig. 1. From the church of Stanford, Northamptonshire. – Fig. 2. Escutcheon from a pulpit window in Bristol Cathedral (Winston, *Glass-painting*). – Fig. 3. From a window in Salisbury Cathedral (Winston). – Fig. 4. From York Cathedral (Christmann, *Kunstgeschichtliches Musterbuch*). – Fig. 5. From a window in the church of Llaurhaidr, Denbighshire (Winston). – Figs. 6 and 8. Grisaille glass from Salisbury Cathedral (Winston). – Fig. 7. Frieze from Canterbury Cathedral (Christmann). – Figs. 9, 10 and 12. Friezes from Salisbury Cathedral (Winston). Fig. 11. Stucco from Salisbury Cathedral (Lacroix et Seré, *Le moyen âge et la renaissance*).

Plate 64. English medieval sculpture

Figs. 1–5 and 8–16: Details from English tombs. – Fig. 6. Countess Aveline of Lancaster's (d. 1269) tomb in Westminster Abbey. – Fig. 7. The tomb of John Fitz Alan, Earl of Arundel (d. 1434) in the church of Arundel. (Stothard, *The monumental effigies of Great Britain.*)

Plate 65. Italian 13th-century mural painting

Fig. 1. Groin of a vault in the choir of the lower church of St. Francis of Assisi. – Fig. 2. Painted fillet in St. Andrea's, Vercelli. – Fig. 3. Fillet on a pillar in the church of St. Francis of Assisi. Figs. 4 and 8. Frieze and wedge-painting by Giotto in the church of St. Francis of Assisi. – Fig. 5. Pillar with groins of vault painted by Giotto in the upper church of St. Francis of Assisi. – Fig. 6. Ceiling in the same church. – Fig. 7. Painted soffit of an arc in the same church. (Gruner, *Specimens of ornamental art.*)

1.

2.

3.

4.

5.

6.

7.

8.

Plate 66. Italian 14th-century mural painting

Figs. 1–12. Mural paintings in St. Anastasia's, Verona. (Gruner, *Specimens of ornamental art.*)

Plate 67. Italian Gothic marble floors

Figs. 1–3. Parts of the floor in St. Maria's, Trastevere, 12th century (Gruner, *Specimens of ornamental art*). – Figs. 4 and 7. Parts of the floor in the church of Orf San Michele, Florence, 13th century (Hessemer, *Arabische und altbyzantinische Bauverzierungen*). Figs. 5, 6 and 8. Parts of the floor in St. Maria's, Cosmedia, Rome (Hessemer); these floors made of red porphyry and green serpentine, granite, marble, etc. were to be found in the majority of the churches of Rome during the 12th and 13th century. – Fig. 9. Parts of the floor in the baptistery in Pisa, 12th century (Hessemer). – Fig. 10. Part of the floor in Orvieto Cathedral, 14th century (Hessemer).

1. 2. 3. 4. 5. 6. 9. 7. 10. 8.

Plate 68. Italian Gothic miniature painting

Figs. 1 and 10. Latin initials from the 13th century. – Figs. 2–4, 6, 7, 12, 13 and 15–17. Initials from the 15th century (*Paleographia artistica di Monte Cassino*). – Figs. 5, 8, 11, 14 and 18. Initials from the 13th century (Monte Cassino) – Fig. 9. Initial with Petrarca's portrait from the 14th century (Lacroix et Seré, *Le moyen âge et la renaissance*).

Plate 69. Italian 14th-century silk

Fig. 1. Silk drapery from St. Mary's, Danzig, containing oriental elements. – Figs. 2 and 6. Silk brocade from festive garments in the Provincial Museum, Danzig. – Fig. 3. Silk brocade in the Austrian Museum. – Fig. 4. Silk with Saracenic elements. – Fig. 5. Silk brocade from St. Mary's, Danzig. (Lessing, *Gewebe des Kgl. Kunstgewerbemuseums Berlin*.)

1 4   2 5   3 6

Plate 70. German Gothic ceiling and mural painting

Figs. 1–4 and 11. Paintings from the Cistercian Abbey in Maulbronn (Württemberg), 14th century. – Fig. 5. Ceiling from St. Wolfgang's church near Grades (Austria), beginning of the 16th century. – Fig. 6. Ceiling from the upper choir in the church at Ottmarsheim (Upper Alsace), 14th century. – Figs. 7 and 8. Painting in the soffits in St. Pancratius' chapel in the castle of Tyrol near Meran, 14th century. Fig. 9. From St. James' church near Tramin (Tyrol), 14th century. – Fig. 10. From the monastery church of Wienhausen near Celle, beginning of the 14th century. – Fig. 12. From the church at Büchen (Lauenberg). – Fig. 13. Painted wooden ceiling from St. Valentius' church at Chechlau (Silesia), 1517. (Borrmann, *Aufnahmen mittelalterlicher Wand- und Deckenmalereien in Deutschland.*)

Plate 71. German Gothic miniature painting

Figs. 1, 2, 6 and 18. Initials from a Bible in the Royal Library, Stuttgart, 14th century (Petzendorfer, *Schriftenatlas.*) – Figs. 3, 5, 7, 9, 10, 12–14, 17, 19 and 20. Initials from manuscripts of the 15th century (Petzendorfer). – Figs. 4 and 15. Initials from Austrian manuscripts from the 15th century (Hrackovina, *Initials, Alphabets etc.*). – Figs. 8, 11 and 16. From missals of the 13th, century (Petzendorfer).

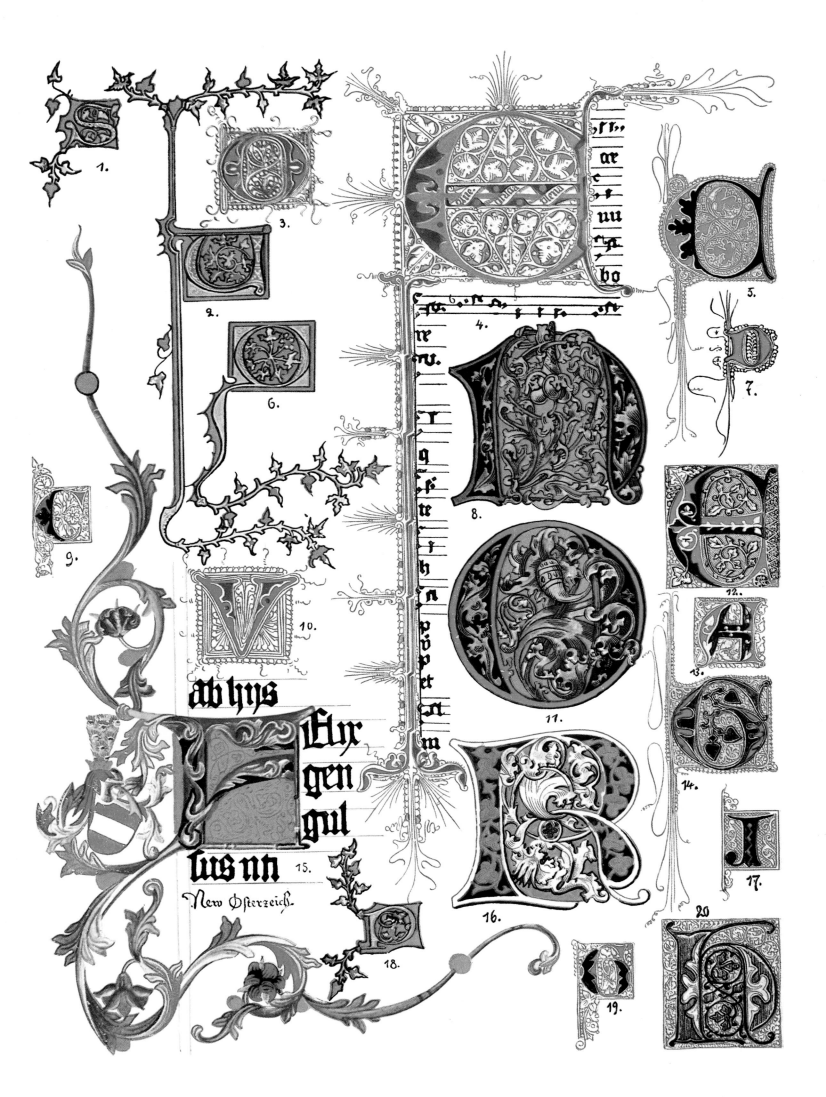

Plate 72. German Gothic glass-painting

Figs. 1–3. From the choir in the monastery church in Königsfelden (Switzerland), mid-14th century. Fig. 4. From St. Catherine's, Oppenheim, 14th century. – Fig. 5. From a window in Ulm Cathedral, 1480. – Figs. 6–8, 13 and 14. In the (Royal) Bavarian National Museum, Munich. – Figs. 9 and 12. Gothic carved work from the 14th century. – Fig. 10. In the Municipal Museum in Cologne, 14th century. – Fig. 11. Window from the Löwenburgkapelle on Wilhelmshöhe near Kassel, 14th century.

Plate 73. Italian Renaissance mural painting

Fig. 1. Vestibule in the Palazzo Imperiale, Piazza Competto, Genoa (Reinhardt, *Genoa*). – Fig. 2. Frieze from the Palazzo Vitelli alla Connoniera, Citta di Castello, dating from the 16th century (Ewald, *Farbige Dekorationen*). – Fig. 3. Mural from Cardinal Bibiena's bathroom in the Vatican, painted by Raffael d'Urbino (Gruber, *Specimens of ornamental art*). – Fig. 4. Wall-decoration from the Palazzo del Toscana in Mantua, painted by G. Romano, about 1530 (Gruber). – Fig. 5. Wall-decoration of Stonza d'Orfeo in the same palace, by the same artist.

Plate 74. Italian Renaissance vault decoration

Fig. 1. Decorations of a vault in the Uffizi Gallery, Florence, from the 16th century (Ewald, *Farbige Dekorationen*). – Fig. 2. Decoration of a vault of Raphael's loggias in the Vatican, Rome, 1516 (Letarouilly, *Le vatican et la sainte basilique de Rome*). – Fig. 3. From the loggia in the Palazzo Andrea Doria, Genoa (Reinhardt, *Genoa*). – Figs. 4 and 5. Decorations of vaults on the second floor of Raphael's loggias in the Vatican, 1516 (Letarouilly).

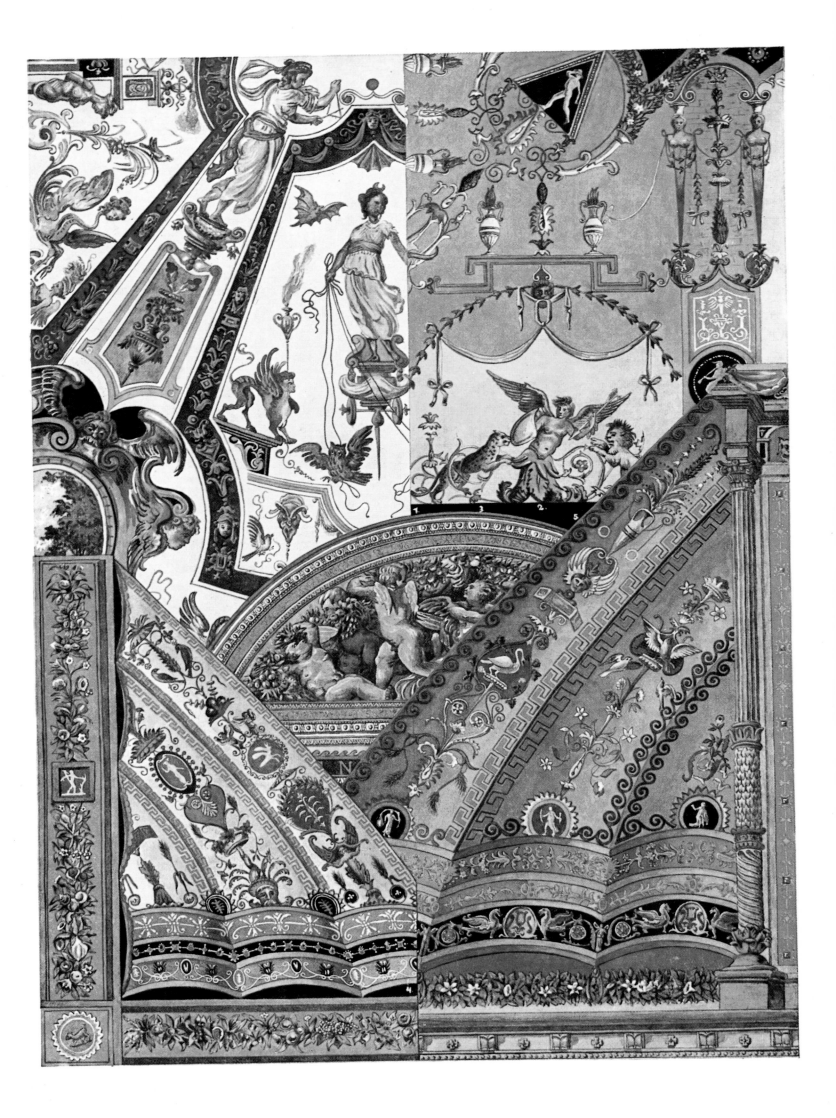

Plate 75. Italian majolica tiles

Figs. 1–3. Majolica tiles from Siena and Amalfi, 15th century (Meurer, *Italienische Majolikafliesen*). – Fig. 4. Collection of tiles from two Genoese palaces in Nilo San Matteo and Via Luccoli (Herdtle, *Eine Sammlung italienischer Majolikafliesen*).

Plate 76. Italian majolica ware

Figs. 1–3. Vinegar bottles. (Delange und Bornemann, *Recueil des fayences Italiennes*). – Fig. 2. Vase from Urbino from the middle of the 16th century; in one of its cartouches Apollo pursuing Daphne with Diana in the sky (Spitzer collection). – Fig. 4. Small vase from Urbino, 1540 (Spitzer collection). – Fig. 6. Salt-cellar from the studio of Patanazzi, Urbino, 1560 (Spitzer collection). – Fig. 7. Vase made by Marc Antonio Patanazzi, Urbino, 1580 (Spitzer collection). – Fig. 8. Salt-cellar from Urbino, 1550 (Spitzer collection).

Plate 77. Italian Renaissance glass

Fig. 1. Jug from the 16th century (Nesbitt, *A descriptive catalogue of the glass vessels in the South Kensington Museum*). – Figs. 2 and 5. Glass bowls from the 15th century (Spitzer collection). – Figs. 3, 4 and 6. Glass bottles from the 15th century (Spitzer collection). – Figs. 7, 8 and 11. Wine glasses from the 15th century (Spitzer collection). – Figs. 9 and 10. Enamelled glass cups, in the Kunstgewerbemuseum, Berlin (Lehnert, *Illustrierte Geschichte des Kunstgewerbes*).

Plate 78. Italian Renaissance jewellery

Fig. 1. Key. – Figs. 2, 16 and 19. Pendants. – Fig. 3. Glass pendant. – Fig. 4. Pendant with cameo representing Leda and the swan. – Fig. 5. Pendant cross made of crystal and jasper. – Fig. 6. Engraved sardonyx medallion. – Fig. 7. Small dish of enamelled copper showing the adoration of the Magi. – Fig. 8. Cameo. – Figs. 9, 12, 13, and 18. Outer case of a watch. – Fig. 10. Pendant with the annunciation. – Fig. 11. Pendant. – Figs. 14, 15, and 20. Medallions. – Fig. 17. Pendant with painted wax portrait. (Spitzer collection.)

Plate 79. Italian Renaissance tarsia

Figs. 1 and 7. From stalls in St. Maria Novella, Florence (Meurer, *Italienische Flachornamente*). – Fig. 2. From a stall in St. Maria in Organo, Verona (Gruber, *Specimens of ornamental art*). – Figs. 3 and 5. From a stall in St. Maria's in Organo, Verona (Meurer). – Fig. 4. From a stall in Certosa near Pavia (Meurer). – Fig. 6. From a stall in St. Mark's, Venice (Meurer).

1

3

2

4

5

6

7

Plate 80. Italian Renaissance inlaid marble

Figs. 1, 2, 6, 7, and 8. Marble tarsia from Padua (Weissbachsche Sammlung in der Kunstgewerbebibliothek, Dresden). Fig. 3. Marble tarsia from Certosa near Pavia (Weißbachsche Sammlung). – Fig. 4. Marble tarsia from St. Domenico, Messina (Weißbachsche Sammlung). – Fig. 5. Marble tarsia in the Museum Pio Clementino, Rome.

Plate 81. Italian Renaissance miniature painting

Figs. 1, 3, and 4. From Italian prayer books (Spitzer collection) – Figs 2, 6, and 7. From Italian manuscripts (Wyatt, *The art of illuminating as practised in Europe from the earliest times*). – Fig. 4. Initial copied from Professor Borchard, Stuttgart.

Plate 82. Italian silk and velvet

Figs. 1, 3, and 8. North Italian silk (Fischbach, *Gewebe*). – Fig. 2. Italian silk (Dupont-Auberville, *L'ornement des tissus*). – Figs. 4, 5 and 9. Venetian velvet and brocade (Fischbach). – Figs. 6 and 7. Genoese velvet (Fischbach).

1.

2.

3.

4.

5.

6.

7.

8.

9.

Plate 83. French Renaissance mural painting

Figs. 1–6 and 8–11. Mural painting in the Château de Blois. – Fig. 7. Wall decoration in the chapel of the Château de Blois. (Le Nail, *Château de Blois*.)

Plate 84. Painted wood ceilings in France

Figs. 1 and 2. Ceilings from the Château de Videville (Seine et Oise) from the time of Louis XIII. – Fig. 3. Box ceiling from the room of the assizes, Dijon, from the time of Francis I. – Fig. 4. Box ceiling in the Château d'Auet from the time of Henry II. – Fig. 5. Decorated beams in the Château de Videville. (Daly, *Motifs historiques*.)

1

2.

3

4.

5.

6

Plate 85. Stoneware from Oiron

Fig. 1. Dish from the Duke of Hamilton's collection, England. – Fig. 2. Dish from Mr. H. Delange's collection. – Fig. 3. Jug from Mr. Hope's collection, London. – Fig. 4. Jug from Mr. Andrew Fountaine's collection, England. – Fig. 5. Chandelier from Baron Anthony Rothschild's collection, London, – Fig. 6. Inside of a dish from Baron Anthony Rothschild's collection. – Fig. 7. Salt-cellar from Count of Passau's collection in Airvault.
(Delange, *Recueil des fayences françaises dites de Henry II et de Diane de Poitiers*.)

Plate 86. Pallissy faience

Figs. 1 and 3. Triangular salt-cellars (Spitzer collection). – Fig. 2. Vinegar bottle (Spitzer collection). – Fig. 4. Dish showing Bachus' childhood (Lacroix et Serré, *Le moyen âge et la renaissance*). – Fig. 5. Jug (Spitzer collection). – Figs. 6 and 8. Dish for a vinegar bottle (Spitzer collection). – Fig. 7. Dish (Lacroix et Serré). – Figs. 9 and 11. Plate (Spitzer collection). – Fig. 10. Large oval plate.

Plate 87. Limoges enamel

Fig. 1. Enamel picture, signed Shif (Spitzer collection). – Fig. 2. Dish made by Pierre Reymond in Limoges, dating from the second half of the 16th century (Lehnert, *Geschichte des Kunstgewerbes*). – Fig. 3. Plate made by Jean de Court (Spitzer collection). – Figs. 4 and 6. Vessels made by Jean Courteys (Spitzer collection). – Fig. 5. Cashbox made by Penicaud (Spitzer collection).

Plate 88. French Renaissance goldsmiths' work

Fig. 1. Timepiece from the Sauvageot collection, Paris, 16th century (Lacroix et Serré, *Le moyen âge et la renaissance*). – Fig. 2. Dish with Limoges enamel made by Pierre Reymond (Wyatt, *Metalwork*). – Fig. 3. Dish with cameos, 17th century (Havard, *Dictionnaire de l'ameublement et de la décoration*). – Figs. 4 and 7. Watches from the Sauvageot collection, Paris, 16th century (Lacroix). – Fig. 5. Dish made of lapis lazuli in gilded silver setting in the Gallery Apollo, Paris, 17th century (Havard). – Fig. 6. Censer in the Museum of Cluny, 17th century (Wyatt). – Fig. 8. Vinegar jug in the Louvre, Paris, 16th century (Wyatt).

Plate 89. French Renaissance miniature painting

Fig. 1. Cameo painting from a prayer book of Henry II in the Bibliothèque Nationale, Paris (Lacroix et Serré, *Le moyen âge et la renaissance*). – Fig. 2. Page of a prayer book from the 16th century (Spitzer collection). – Fig. 3. Marginal ornament of a manuscript of Mathias Corvin from the 16th century in the Bibliothèque Nationale, Paris, depicting Francis I (Lacroix et Serré).

1

2

3.

2.

4.

LEX: qm exaudiet do
minus uoce oronis mee
ma inchnauit aurem suam mi

Plate 90. French velvet and silk

Figs. 1 and 2. Velvet (Dupont-Auberville, *L'ornement des tissus*). – Figs. 3, 9, 10, and 11. Silk (Dupont-Auberville). – Figs. 4 and 6. Silk (Fischbach, *Ornamente der Gewebe*). – Fig. 5. Silk (Fischbach). – Figs. 7 and 8. Satin (Dupont-Auberville).

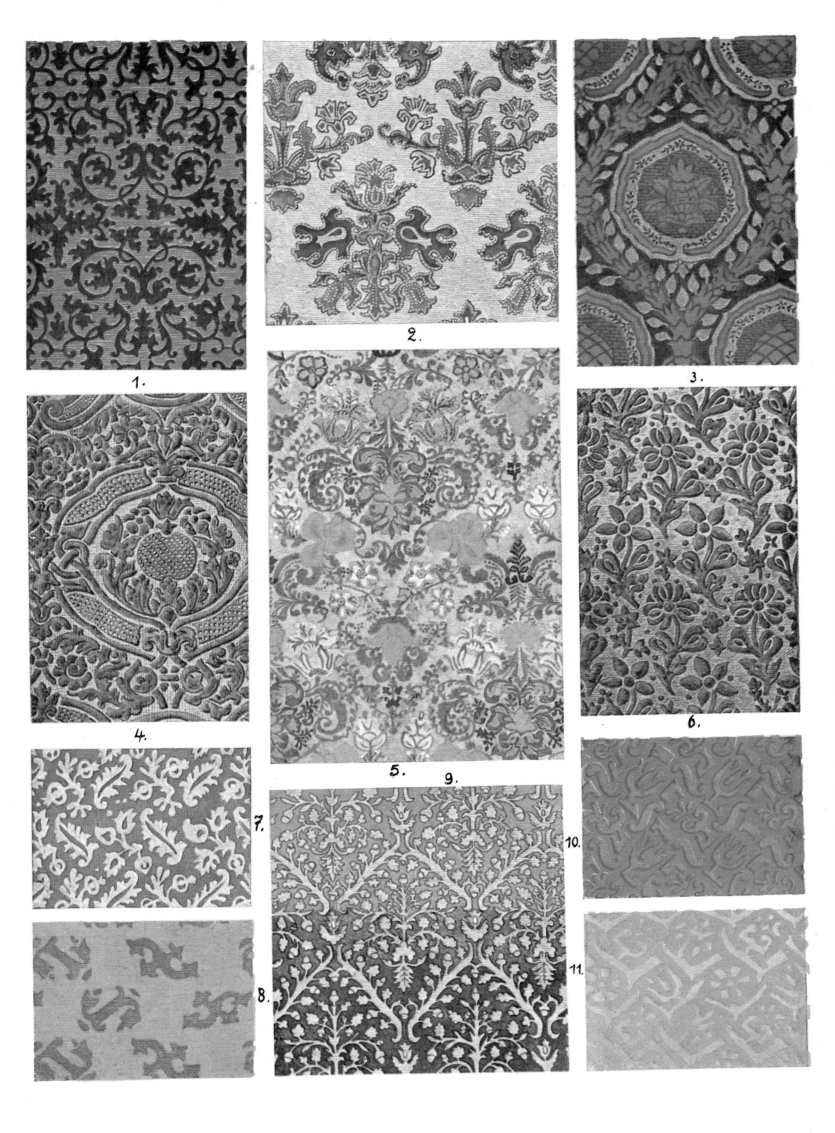

1.

2.

3.

4.

5.

6.

7.

8.

9.

10.

11.

Plate 91. French Renaissance embroidery

Fig. 1. Embroidery of Henry II's bed (Dupont-Auberville, *L'ornament du tissus*). – Fig. 2. Coif from the 16th century (Lacroix et Serré, *Le moyen âge et la renaissance*). – Fig. 3. Table-cloth with ornaments of black velvet on a background of white satin (Dupont-Auberville). – Fig. 4. From royal bed canopies (Dupont-Auberville). – Figs. 5, 6, 9, 10, 12, 13, 14 and 16. Various embroideries (Dupont-Auberville). – Figs. 7, 8, 11 and 15. Various lace work (Racinet, *L'ornement polychrome*).

Plate 92. Painted wooden ceilings of the German Renaissance

Figs. 1 and 3. Painted ceilings in Castle Neuhaus in Bohemia, 16th century (Ewald, *Farbige Dekorationen*). – Fig. 2. From the ceiling of the Hall of the Knights in Castle Heiligenberg.

1

3

2

Plate 93. German Renaissance wall decoration

View of the northern wall and door in the Reiche Kapelle in the Royal Residence, Munich. (Enzler, Zettler, and Dr. Stockbauer, *Ausgewählte Kunstwerke aus dem Schatze der Reichen Kapelle in der Königlichen Residenz, München.*)

Plate 94. German Renaissance jewellery

Figs. 1, 7, 10, 17, 18, 19, 22, 23, 25 and 27. Jewellery from the Spitzer collection, Paris. – Fig. 2. Link of a chain in a painting in the Royal Gallery, Kassel (Luthmer, *Goldschmuck der Renaissance*). – Fig. 3. Button from the Royal Treasury, Berlin (Luthmer). – Fig. 4. A bridal chain in a painting in the Germanisches Museum, Nuremberg (Luthmer). – Fig. 5. Ring (Luthmer). – Fig. 6. Brooch (Luthmer). – Fig. 8. Pendant in a painting by H. Baldung Grien, Woerlitz (Luthmer). – Figs. 9 and 20. Buttons in a painting in the castle of Schleissheim (Luthmer). – Fig. 11. Necklace in a portrait in the castle of Gotha (Luthmer). – Fig. 12. Pendant in the Bayrisches Nationalmuseum, Munich (Luthmer). – Fig. 13. Pendant on the monstrance in Münster Cathedral, Freiburg, Baden (Luthmer). – Fig. 14. Button from a painting by de Wite in Schleissheim (Luthmer). Fig. 15. Pendant in a painting in Woerlitz (Luthmer). – Fig. 16. Centre-piece from the 16th century in the Museum of the Hall door, Brussels (Lacroix et Serré, *Le moyen âge et la renaissance*). – Fig. 21. Pendant in a portrait in the Städtisches Museum, Cologne (Luthmer). – Fig. 24. Hat-button in a painting in the Royal Gallery, Kassel (Luthmer). – Fig. 26. Cross from the Herzogliches Museum, Gotha (Luthmer). – Fig. 28. Reliquary (Luthmer).

Plate 95. German glass and rock crystal

Figs. 1 and 6. 'Wiederkomm' (leave-taking) glasses by Jakob Braun, Nuremberg (Nesbitt, *Catalogue of the collection of glass formed by Felix Slade*). – Fig. 2. Beer glass with the inscription *'Das Heilige römische Reich mit sampt seinen Gliedern'* (The Holy Roman Empire and all its dominions), 1572 (Nesbitt). – Fig. 3. 'Wiederkomm' glass in the South Kensington Museum, 1616 (Nesbitt, *A descriptive catalogue of glass vessels in the Kensington Museum*). – Fig. 4. Rock-crystal cup with lid in the Grünes Gewölbe, Dresden (Gruner, *The green vaults in Dresden*). – Fig. 5. Rock-crystal jug in the Grünes Gewölbe, Dresden (Gruner).

Plate 96. German Renaissance glass painting

Fig. 1. Window from St. Peter's, Cologne, 1530 (Kolb, *Glasmalereien des Mittelalters und der Renaissance*). – Figs. 2 and 4. From St. Peter's, Cologne, 1528 (Schaefer und Roßteuscher, *Monumentale Glasmalereien des Mittelalters und der Renaissance*). – Fig. 3. Part of the 'Tucherfenster' (presented by the Tucher family) in St. Laurentius', Nuremberg, 1601 (Kolb). – Fig. 5. Window with escutcheons in the Germanisches Museum, Nuremberg, 1548 (Kolb). – Fig. 6. Window in the Städtisches Museum, Cologne, 1538 (Kolb). – Fig. 7. Window from Cologne Cathedral, 16th century (Kolb).

Heinrich grebel · 1548

WIALT ZO SCHIF

1   2 3
4   5   7
6

Plate 97. Renaissance ceramics

Figs. 1, 2 and 6. Rhenish jugs (Bach, *Renaissance*). – Fig. 3. Jug from the 16th century *(Kunst und Gewerbe, 1880)*. – Figs. 4, 5 and 7. Clay jugs (Lacroix et Serré, *Le moyen âge et la Renaissance*). – Fig. 8. Beer-jug (Lacroix et Serré). – Fig. 9. Glazed stone jug in the Kunstgewerbemuseum, Berlin.

Plate 98. German book binding

Fig. 1. Stamped binding for Luther's works in the Wittenberg edition from 1556–59, with Luther's portrait. – Fig. 2. Stamped binding with the portrait of Emperor Maximilian II and the year 1583. – Figs. 3 and 4. Front and back of a Saxon binding from the second half of the 16th century. (Lemperts, *Bilderatlas zur Geschichte des deutschen Buchhandels.*)

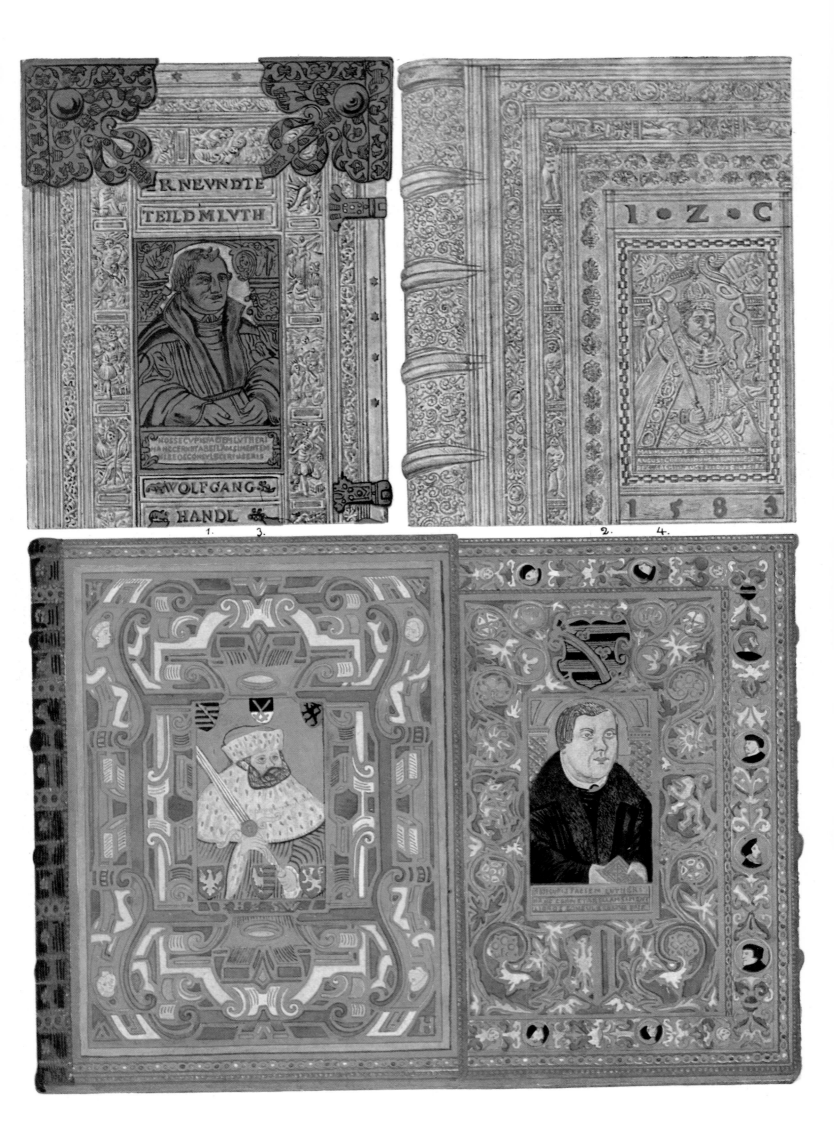

1. 2.
3. 4.

Plate 99. German Renaissance tapestry

Fig. 1. Tapestry representing the arrival of the image of the Holy Virgin from Sablons in Brussels in Charles V's presence, 1518 (Spitzer collection). – Fig. 2. Tapestry in the Mobiliar National. (Guffrey, *Histoire de la tapisserie*).

Plate 100. Spanish and Portuguese tapestry

Figs. 1, 2, 4 and 6. Spanish brocade (Dupont-Auberville, *L'ornement du tissus*). – Fig. 2. Fragment of a tunic from the 16th century (Spitzer collection). – Fig. 5. Carpet with silk and gold embroidery on velvet, Portuguese work from the 16th century (Spitzer collection). – Figs. 7, 8, 9 and 11. Spanish silk (Fischbach, *Ornamente der Gewebe*). – Fig. 16. Spanish embroidery from the 16th century (Spitzer collection).

1.   2.

3.

4.   5.

6.

7.   9.

10

11.   8.

Plate 101. French Baroque interior decoration

Figs. 1 and 2. Painted panelling in the Museum of Decorative Arts, Paris (Ewald, *Farbige Dekorationen*). Figs. 3 and 5. Wall and ceiling decoration in the Institute Pompée, Ivry sur Seine (Daly, *Motifs historiques*). – Fig. 4. Ceiling decoration from the throne-room at Fontainebleau (Ewald).

1   3   2   4   5

Plate 102. Boule furniture

Figs. 1 and 3. Furniture from the *garde mobilier* in Paris (Procinet, *L'ornement poly-chrome*). – Fig. 2. Cabinet. – Fig. 4. Table in the Reiche Kapelle in the Royal Residence, Munich (Enzler, Zettler, and Dr. Stockbauer, *Ausgewählte Kunstwerke aus dem Schatze der Reichen Kapelle in der Königlichen Residenz, München*).

1

3

2

4

Plate 103. French Baroque faience

Figs. 1–4. Plate from Rouen (*Histoire de la fayence de Rouen*). – Fig. 5. Vinegar jug from Rouen with escutcheon of Bishop Froulag-Peffé de Maus (*Histoire de la Fayence de Rouen*). – Fig. 6. Plate in Persian style from the end of the second and the beginning of the third period, 1650–1680 (Broc de Segange, *La fayence et les fayencistes et les emailleurs de Nevers*). – Fig. 7. Chimney ornament from Rouen (*Histoire de la Fayence de Rouen*). – Figs. 8 and 10. Plate from Rouen (*Histoire de la Fayence de Rouen*). – Fig. 9. Holy-water font, attributed to Rodrigue de Duplessis, 1734 (Broc de Segange). Fig. 11. Salt-cellar from Rouen (*Histoire de la Fayence de Rouen*). – Fig. 12. Ornament from a rectangular plate from Rouen (*Histoire de la Fayence de Rouen*). Fig. 13. Tureen in Persian style from the second and third period (Broc de Segange).

Plate 104. Dutch ceramic tiles

Plate 105. Delft faience

Fig. 1. Plate with the arms of Frederic the Great from the collection of Dr. Mandl, Paris (Havard, *Histoire de la fayence de Delft*). – Fig. 2. Plate in the same collection (Ris Paquot, *Histoire générale de la fayence ancienne française et étrangère*). – Fig. 3. Plate in the collection of Rosot, Abbeville (Ris Paquot). – Figs. 4 and 6. Violin in blue cameo in the J. F. London collection at the Haag (Havard). – Fig. 5. Plate in blue cameo by Friedrich van Frytom (Havard). – Figs. 7 and 9. Tiles with the arms of the House of Orange by Piet Vizeer in the J. F. London collection (Havard). – Fig. 8. Border of a plate in the collection of Dr. Mandl, Paris (Ris Paquot).

1.   2.   3.

4.   7.   5.   9.   6.

8.

Plate 106. English late Renaissance furniture

Fig. 1. Chair from the time of James I in the Gallery at Knole House. – Figs. 2 and 3. Chair and back of the chair in Fig. 7. – Figs. 4 and 8. Chair and seat of a chair from the time of William III. – Fig. 5. Chair in the state-room of Hardwicke Hall, Derbyshire, from the time of William III. – Fig. 6. Canopy of a bed from the time of James II. – Fig. 7. Couch from the time of William III.

Plate 107. French Rococo interior decoration

Figs. 1 and 3. Decoration of the ministers' council-hall, Fontainebleau, executed in 1743 by Carl van Loo and François Boucher (Gélis-Didot, *La peinture décorative en France du XVIe au XVIIIe siècle*). – Fig. 2. Decoration made of carved, painted and gilded wood in the saloon of the Hôtel Koquelaure, Paris (Havard, *Dictionnaire de l'ameublement*). – Figs. 4, 6, 7 and 8. Decoration of the ministers' council-hall, Fontainebleau, executed by Pillement (Gehlis-Didot). – Fig. 5. Decoration of a room in the Hôtel Soubise from the beginning of the 18th century.

Plate 108. Sèvres porcelain

Figs. 1 and 4. Sugar boxes. – Figs. 2, 3, 5 and 13. From a dinner-service in the collection of Baron Adolph Rothschild, 1760, painted by Dubois, Parpette, and Mérault jeune. – Fig. 6. Bouquet of a vase, 1757. – Fig. 7. Jug from the M. L. Watelin collection, 1757, painted by Tandart. – Fig. 8. Jug from the collection of the Marquis de Vogué, 1753. – Fig. 9. Vessel and dish from the M. Barre collection, 1755; the dish was painted by Prevost, 1785. – Fig. 10. Plate in the Museum of Decorative Arts, Paris. – Fig. 11. Plate from the L. Watelin collection, painted by Cremont, 1761. – Fig. 12. Coffee-service in the South Kensington Museum. – Fig. 14. Plate from the L. Watelin collection, 1753 (Garmir, *La porcelaine tendre de Sèvres.*)

Plate 109. Baroque and Rococo fabrics

Figs. 1–6, 8 and 9. Lyons silk drapery. – Fig. 7. Damask. (Dupont-Auberville, *L'ornement des tissus.*)

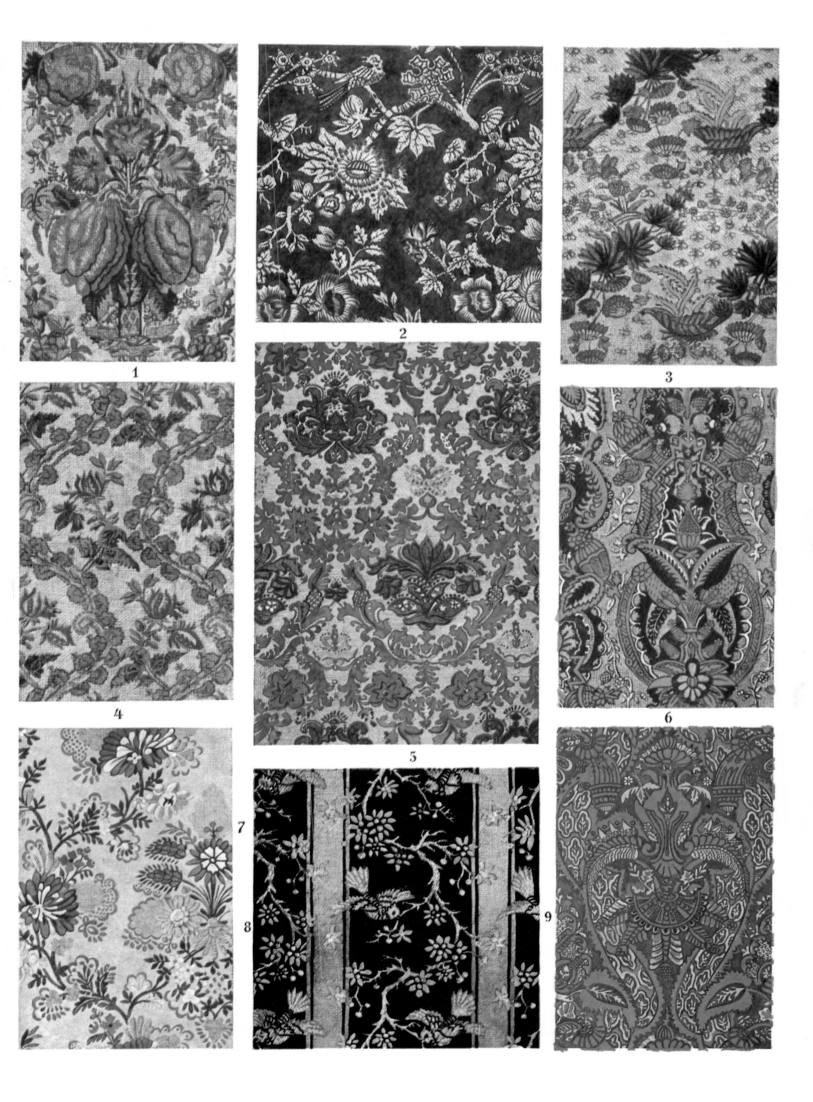

Plate 110. Dresden and Berlin porcelain

Fig. 1. Tureen of the Schwanenservice by Johann Joachim Kändler, Meissen (Lehnert, *Illustrierte Geschichte des Kunstgewerbes*). – Fig. 2. Dish from Frederick the Great's service, 1768 (*Berliner Porzellan*). – Fig. 3. Vase with ornaments, Meissen (Lehnert). – Figs. 4 and 7. From the coffee-service in the Charlottenburger Schloss, Berlin, 1768 (Kunstgewerbemuseum Berlin, Heft 18). – Fig. 5. Vase (*Berliner Porzellan*). – Figs. 6 and 8. From a coffee-service, 1770 (Kunstgewerbemuseum Berlin). – Fig. 9. Dish (*Berliner Porzellan*). – Figs. 10 and 11. Saucers (*Berliner Porzellan*).